BEYOND
THE SCRIPT
drama in the classroom

TAKE TWO

First published April 2004
by the Primary English Teaching Association
Laura Street, Newtown NSW 2042 Australia

Copyright © Primary English Teaching Association 2004

National Library of Australia Cataloguing-in-Publication data

Ewing, Robyn (Robyn Ann), 1955– .
Beyond the script : take 2 : drama in the classroom.

Bibliography.
ISBN 1 875622 56 X

1. Drama in education. 2. Drama – Study and teaching (Primary).
I. Simons, Jennifer. II. Hertzberg, Margery. III. Primary English Teaching
Association (Australia). IV. Title.

372.66044

Cover and internal design by Jane Cameron, Fisheye Design
Edited by Barry Gordon
Printed by Ligare Book Printer, Riverwood
Typeset in Humanist 521 and Trixie

Copying for educational purposes
The Copyright Act 1968 (Cth) allows a maximum of one chapter or 10% of this book, whichever is the greater, to be copied by any educational institution for its educational purposes provided that the educational institution (or the body that administers it) has given a remuneration notice to the Copyright Agency Limited (CAL) under the Act.

Copying for other purposes
Except as permitted under the Act – for example a fair dealing for the purposes of study, research, criticism or review – no part of this book may be reproduced, stored in a retrieval system or transmitted in any form or by any means without prior written permission from the copyright holder.

PETA
Primary English Teaching Association

BEYOND THE SCRIPT
drama in the classroom

TAKE TWO

Robyn Ewing
& Jennifer Simons
with Margery Hertzberg

CONTENTS

	Prologue	1
1	What is educational drama?	3
2	A piece of the action: Drama games with a difference	13
3	Getting into it: Movement, mime and still image	23
4	Exploring teacher in role and mantle of the expert	31
5	Programming using drama strategies and literary texts	39
6	Puppetry	53
7	Playbuilding	59
8	Storying	71
9	Readers' theatre	83
10	Drama when English is an additional language	93
11	Evaluation and assessment	109
12	Taking shape: Aesthetics and drama form	117
	Epilogue	125
	Brief glossary	127
	Selected further drama references	129

Wolf came to class. he had a Shadow & Brown fur. He had a point y ears. Likes to play tennis. eats little Pigs.

PROLOGUE

Sometimes the director of a film isn't completely happy with the first take. There may be another angle to consider — perhaps a different perspective on a character, or a new light on a particular scene. The first edition of *Beyond the Script* was our initial attempt to document theories and practices about the teaching of drama that we had individually taught in the classroom and then, together, developed with our tertiary students and workshopped with teachers.

Since that time, seven years ago, many of our colleagues and preservice teachers have told us how helpful the book has been as a starting point. But they've asked for more. This, then, is our second 'take' on what has now been almost 15 years of collaboration. While many of the ideas and examples in this edition are new, we remain passionately committed to the central belief that drama is a powerful teaching and learning methodology across the curriculum, as well as an art form in its own right. Used well, drama will help your students to develop empathy, challenging them to consider how others think, feel and respond to the world. They will explore who they are, and they will improve their talking, listening, reading and writing skills. This edition will provide you with further support for that enterprise.

Experimenting with drama is a risk. You are challenging conventional classroom roles and relationships. You are not always able to predict where the drama will go. Newcomers to drama may initially get overexcited and confused, so it's important to establish rules and expectations. The best learning occurs within a supportive classroom environment in which students are challenged to think beyond the square and encouraged to connect with what's happening in their world. Students need to know that it's OK to have a go and make mistakes, and that you are a co-learner on the journey.

In this edition, we've drawn on more recent research and on our own experiences in classrooms, along with the work of many teachers and students. Many of the examples are new. Margery Hertzberg has written a significant new chapter on using drama with multilingual students. We have also included a glossary of drama devices used throughout the book.

We feel enormously privileged that PETA has given us the opportunity to revise the book and that Barry Gordon, editor extraordinaire, agreed to edit it. The principal, Trish Cavenagh, and all the teachers and students at Curl Curl North primary school in Sydney also deserve special thanks. For the last nine years the school has worked in partnership with the University of Sydney's Faculty of Education and Social Work to explore authentic texts through drama, with the aim of enhancing students' literacy. Many of the examples and photos are drawn from this experience. We are also grateful to all our students, current and past, because it is they who have helped us to extend, adapt and develop our ideas on the critical role that drama can and should play in the classroom.

Have fun!

Robyn Ewing
Jennifer Simons

Faculty of Education and Social Work
University of Sydney

CHAPTER ONE

What is educational drama?

Most people think they know what drama is. But when it's applied to the purpose of education, a range of views emerges, often arising out of experiences at school. Over the years we've regularly asked our preservice teachers to tell us what educational drama is. Responses like "acting" are common. For some, however, the essence of drama lies in playing fun games, charades or 'skits'. Others see it as the reading of plays or the performing of scripts for an audience. While all of these associations reflect aspects of educational drama, they do not capture its essence. We aim to do that in this chapter, focusing on the use of drama in primary- and middle-school classrooms.

Describing educational drama

Drama in education is both a *method* of teaching/learning and a *body of knowledge* in its own right. Essentially it's about *enactment*: using the body in time and space to explore issues, questions, perspectives or ideas.

Process drama

One of the most important forms of educational drama is *process* drama. Its purpose is to "establish an imagined world, a dramatic 'elsewhere' created by the participants as they discover, articulate, and sustain fictional roles and situations" (O'Neill, 1995:xvi).

Students develop their understanding of this imagined world through the same meaning-making processes that they use in everyday life: they interpret body language and voice qualities; read emotions; explore subtexts; respond to what they think other people want; manipulate symbols; and use particular values to make a decision, choose from alternative actions and evaluate the consequences of that choice. They do so in an imagined world that they create together. Groups of students collaborate in role to express and explore ideas. There is no outside audience and no intention to communicate beyond the participants themselves. So, although the participants work in role, their acting ability is not usually important: all that is needed is that the participants willingly suspend their disbelief.

In process drama, the students are generally viewed as social beings; the objective is to pursue an understanding of the society they live in. Your teaching role is to facilitate this pursuit, creating a space where 'radical tolerance' is the goal:

> **This is not a form of tolerance that simply allows us to 'put up with' the existence of multiple forms of life and world views. Rather, it aims at a mutual recognition and co-understanding** *(Mayerfeld Bell & Gardiner, 1998:6).*

The topics explored by drama can come from many curriculum areas. Drama can be used, for example, to investigate the effects of war on a society (Studies in Society). Improvisation can facilitate the use of conversational language for new speakers of English (TESOL). Role-play can be used to develop an understanding of numbers or space, or of a chemical reaction (Mathematics and Science).

One of the most fruitful learning areas for drama is that of English. For example, hot-seating (often called questioning in role) can be used to examine a particular literary character's motives. Keeping a journal in role as a minor character can assist students to see an event from a perspective different from the narrator's. Through making a map or a diagram for the drama, students can be led to more critical interrogation of the text.

Drama has many different faces in the classroom. Sometimes students perform prepared scripts in front of others. Sometimes the teacher joins with the group to improvise in role. Sometimes students work in pairs or small groups, preparing and then sharing their improvisations or depictions with the whole class. Sometimes they remain very still — thinking, planning or reflecting. At other times, they draw or write in role, or research aspects of the past in the library.

Planning drama lessons

To ensure a good drama lesson, your plan needs to include several important components of the art form of drama: **role**, **focus**, **tension** and **symbol**. Each of these is introduced below.

Role

If the essence of educational drama is enactment, the way to enactment is to step into another person's shoes. By taking this step, students learn to assume roles that are both similar to and different from those of their real lives, temporarily adopting another person's perspective. They use their bodies to explore the consequences of thinking in this way, maintaining their stance as other members of the class, in different roles, interact with them. As Harper Lee wrote in *To Kill a Mockingbird*, none of us can ever really understand another until we have had the opportunity to "climb into his skin and walk around in it".

It's important that you are also prepared to take on a role within a fictional event. You may first need to demonstrate how that's done — moving in and out of role so that the students can see that sometimes you are pretending to be, say, the Wicked Witch or an advertising executive, and sometimes stepping out of role and speaking as the teacher. Your students may also need to try walking around the room, coming in and out of role, so that they can understand the differences between the character and themselves.

Some personalities can accept fiction and pretence more readily than others. There is a whole range of reasons for this: for instance, some people prefer staying anchored in the 'real' world and find it quite frightening, difficult or embarrassing to move into a fictional world. Thus, when you're introducing drama, you may need to spend some time allowing students to learn that adopting a role is non-threatening, and that what happens in the drama has no consequences outside it.

Moving into role

One of the most important concepts of drama is *protection into role*. This doesn't mean avoiding emotion, but structuring the work so that students are able to explore emotions safely. If a distance is established between the students' reality and the fiction, they are saved from confusing the fictional world with distressing elements of reality. The roles they adopt should clearly differ from themselves. For example, you can move their ages up several years and spend time establishing the fictional background. You can ask them to name and draw their setting. If it's a school, it can be placed in a different part of the country so that they're not obviously talking about their real school. If the material is 'hot' (i.e. potentially threatening), then detached, more contemplative techniques like tableaux are preferable to real-time improvisation.

Improvisation

Drama can be seen as a form of game-playing, and students need to understand its rules before they can participate. Not everything is planned, and one of the rules for working in role is *improvising* — thinking on one's feet. The essence of improvisation is spontaneity. In everyday life, much of what we do is fairly predictable. However, when confronted by unexpected events we act spontaneously, drawing on our intuition, imagination and perhaps our past experiences of similar events.

To improvise successfully, students have to respond to 'offers' of action — statements with embedded suggestions of context or character that can be taken up or rejected. They need to be able to pick up and elaborate on contextual cues, some of which can be very subtle. For example, if you say "Oh, Humpty Dumpty, you look a bit broken up there — what's happened to you?", the student addressed has to be able to recognise the allusion to the nursery rhyme and quickly give a matching response (e.g. "I fell off the wall"). Depending on students' background knowledge of culture or stories, they may need to have a class discussion and pooling of ideas before improvising. However, if you're confident that the students have sufficient background information[>], they may enjoy an abrupt leap into the drama world.

> > The PETA book What's the Story? *(Lowe, 2002)* discusses this background knowledge in terms of self-experience, world experience and knowledge of texts.

Making an offer

Working in role is a collaborative exercise in which participants build a composite picture of the imagined world, negotiating its reality as the characters interact. Drama depends on students being able to accept each other's 'offers'. Although any participant's line of dialogue or action (i.e. any 'offer') may be rejected, a particularly solid rejection may block the drama. For example, if the offer "You're wearing a green dress" is met with a response like "It's not green, it's red", that could finish the drama. The students may need to be taught how to accept an offer, or how to disagree without blocking — for example: "Oh, you think this is green? Through my sunglasses it looks red." It's also possible to accept part of the offer and adjust some of the details, as in: "No, take those green-coloured glasses off — they're affecting your sight".

Levels of role

Different levels of role are used in educational drama, and it's important for students to have some understanding of them. Five levels have been distinguished by Morgan and Saxton (1987), and they are summarised below.

1. **Dramatic playing.** Students are themselves in a make-believe situation. For example, early-years students on an imaginary trip to Old Macdonald's farm are not required to be anybody but themselves; they just have to accept the fiction.

2. **Mantle of the expert.** Students speak as if they are 'the ones who know' — perhaps as architects who've designed a new building or as archaeologists who've just dug up a dinosaur bone. This level is explored further in Chapter 4.

3. **Role-playing.** Students adopt somebody else's point of view. At this level, they won't be speaking with an accent, or hobbling with a crooked stick, or trying to make their bodies look other than they naturally are. The focus is *internal* — they take on the attitude of somebody else, speaking and behaving as they believe such a person would speak and behave. They may, for example, take the position of a logger or a conservationist in a discussion about forest management.

4. **Characterising.** Students begin to represent an individual lifestyle. For example, they may characterise an old woman. This differs from *role-playing* an old woman. In characterising, students begin to adopt signs (e.g. articles of clothing or ways of speaking), and they need time to explore some of the different possibilities of representing a role. So, while characterising is appropriate

for prepared drama, like readers' theatre, it may be the wrong level for a real-time improvisation.

5. Acting. Students move from classroom exploration to performing before an audience. They need to give considerable thought to things like costume, make-up, symbolic objects, accent and inflexion, movement, use of space, and so on. The emphasis shifts from enjoying an experience for oneself to creating an experience for the spectator.

Building roles

Roles are built around three important aspects: **function**, **status** and **attitude**.

Each role has a *function* in creating the totality of the drama. Questions such as:

- What is the character trying to achieve?
- How does s/he assist or hinder the others?

can be asked to help students think about a role.

Sometimes roles have only a simple function. If, for example, you're exploring 'The fish netter on the Great Barrier Reef', you may not really care about his or her home life; all that's important is his or her impact on the reef. In an issues-based drama, students don't need to go much deeper than a simple role function. (This might change as the drama goes on, however. For instance, the fish netter might have a change of attitude.)

At other times, *status* is important in role development, particularly when you are also in role. In such cases, questions like these may need to be considered:

- How much power does the character have compared with the other people in the performance?
- Who is the leader?
- Is s/he in danger of being overthrown in this group, or is s/he beyond challenge?

Knowing a character's power will affect choices of vocabulary, posture, gesture and tone of voice. It will also contribute to each character's *attitude* (or emotional position) towards the events being considered in the drama. Questions like:

- What actions are suggested by the attitude?

- What actions will demonstrate it?

will help students to concentrate on attitude as a way of developing a role. For example, when publicly commenting on a contentious issue, a student in role as a radio commentator will make different choices from someone in role as Prime Minister.

Sometimes, of course, actions may not correspond with attitude. For example, Snow White's stepmother *seems* to be presenting a desirable gift when she offers the golden apple. This is an opportunity to explore *subtext* — unwritten dynamics. Before students are able to use subtext successfully, you will generally need to take on and model roles in which there is apparent contradiction between attitude and action. After that, you might explore subtextual tension by asking students to try saying 'Yes' when they mean yes, when they mean maybe, and when they mean no.

Managing and modelling roles

Once students begin to present another person's point of view, the question of stereotyping emerges. How do we know what other people would do or think? Gavin Bolton (1988) has talked about two ways of acting in real life: **modelling** and **managing**.

Modelling involves basing behaviour on past experience and observation — the behaviour of our parents, peers, movie stars etc. *Managing* involves behaviour that's triggered by uncommon circumstances. For example, a traveller in a foreign country often has to face new and challenging situations, and an unfamiliar language. The traveller can't base her or his behaviour on models, because there's no precedent, or life experience, to draw on. Instead, the traveller has to manage — respond, adapt, invent.

The style of drama introduced by Dorothy Heathcote in Britain in the 1960s combined managing and modelling. One example is provided in the 1970s videotape *Building Belief,* a role-play about early American colonists. In the early stages of the lesson, students used modelling — building up their roles using their knowledge of historical characters (such as the Pilgrims) until they felt comfortable. In role as the oldest citizen, Martha Sharp, Heathcote allowed the colonists to divide the land among themselves while she pretended to sleep. Then they were issued with a challenge that they had to deal with in a managing mode: waking up, she angrily demanded them to defend the fact that they hadn't given any land to her.

Focus

Although role can be seen as the essence of drama, a good lesson only results when the work is focused, centring around a worthwhile educational goal. When drama fails, it's often because it's formless or tries to cover too much. All of the great plays have a central focus — a worthwhile theme to which all the events contribute. *The Merchant of Venice*, for example, looks at issues of justice and equity; *The Crucible* examines what can happen when fear overtakes rationality; *Pygmalion* explores the notions of class and language. As the teacher, you need to decide what your focus will be and how drama can help you explore this central issue.

Classroom drama can be focused by introducing an aspect of life that the students know from their own experience. For example, in a drama about bushrangers, students would probably enact a stereotype based on their limited knowledge about bushrangers from films or books. But if the focus is on the *nervous* bushranger, they can bring to the drama a second dimension — one that they have experienced themselves. Their enactments are enriched, and so are the questions that might be explored. For example:

- Do I trust my friends?
- Am I a brave person?

This 'second dimension' is very important for focusing drama work. Bolton, who coined the term, also terms it the 'adjective' of the role — the students play not astronauts but *first-time* astronauts.

Tension

Drama examines the processes of living, which usually involve competing drives or forces. It's when conflict is unresolved — when there's a state of *tension* — that drama exists. Tension produces the excitement, or the 'edge', that engages learners both intellectually and emotionally, and motivates them to become involved in the drama activity.

Lesson planning for drama therefore needs to identify the sources of tension and maintain them. In a simple sense, tension is maintained by postponing the resolution. One or more constraints can serve this purpose. For example, you could change the time frame in which your students are operating: they could become astronauts in space, weightless and only able to walk in very slow motion. With running impossible, they need to work out a different plan for escaping the space monsters. The lesson has a built-in tension — a constraint that is going to delay the resolution of reaching the safety of the spaceship. Alternatively, you might limit space, so that the students have to crawl on hands and knees through a tunnel. This kind of constraint will set up a different kind of tension. In a role-play where characters are arguing, the constraint could be provided in your instructions to the students in role — for example: "I want her to know that you're angry but you're not allowed to put it into words; you can't actually say 'I'm very angry with you'". The students have to try less direct, more ambiguous, methods of communication.

Symbol

Symbolism is the use of one thing to represent another. Drama usually works best if its theme applies at several levels. For instance, a play about the convict era might also represent a timeless conflict between justice and loyalty. To reinforce such general metaphors, objects or events are often used repeatedly in the drama so that they accumulate meaning and emotional connotations. Thus, in a drama about runaways, the family photograph that the girl constantly carries can eventually stand alone to represent her longing for home.

While an object (or a word or movement) may come to have a shared meaning, you can also give students an opportunity to think about what it might symbolise for them individually. For example, an old-fashioned oil lamp placed in the centre of the class circle may symbolise warmth and hope for some students, but for others it may signify something quite different — silence and solitude perhaps.

Reflection and disengagement

Because students use process drama to learn about other people and themselves, it's important that they have a chance to articulate what they've learned, and to compare their experiences with those of others. It's also important that they spend time disengaging from their roles, especially if their emotions have been aroused. You may need to encourage them to talk in a distanced way about the roles they've been playing in order to help them make a clear distinction between fiction and reality. You might focus on the techniques that they used, or ask questions like: "When you were being the werewolf, what did you think about the magician?". This will help students to take a step back from the role. With students in earlier years, this 'step back' could be quite literal: you could encourage them to take an actual step back, or spin around, to signal they have re-entered reality. Another technique involves setting up a narrow space that students have to travel through to get into and out of the drama world.

References and sources

Bolton, G (1988) 'Drama as Art'. *Drama Broadsheet* 5 (3).

Heathcote, D (1974) *Building Belief*. Part 1. Video, 28 mins. Northwestern University Film Library.

Lee, H (1960) *To Kill a Mockingbird*. Heinemann, Portsmouth.

Mayerfeld Bell, M & Gardiner, M (eds) (1998) *Bakhtin and the Human Sciences: No Last Words*. Sage Publications, New York.

Morgan, N & Saxton, J (1987) *Teaching Drama: A Mind of Many Wonders*. Hutchinson, London.

O'Neill, C (1995) *Drama Worlds: A Framework for Process Drama*. Heinemann, Portsmouth.

Wagner, J (1995) *The Werewolf Knight*. Mark Macleod, Sydney.

Warren, K (1991) *Hooked on Drama*. Macquarie University Institute of Early Childhood, Sydney.

Australias largest search engine for rare, antiquarian and out of print books

Books & Collectibles

www.booksandcollectibles.com.au

JULES BOOKS

Used rare and out of print books of all genres bought and sold

Phone: 0424 429448
jules@JulesBooks.com.au
www.JulesBooks.com.au

Private collections purchased
Book search service available

CHAPTER TWO

A piece of the action:
Drama games with a difference

Many teachers believe in the value of games to 'warm up' students or introduce them to some of the essential skills of drama, such as collaboration, focus and the channelling of energy. Watching individuals as they keep (or don't keep!) to the rules of a game, as they lead, follow and/or collaborate, can be useful for determining the level at which to begin drama proper. Moreover, adapting the content of a game to whatever drama theme is about to be explored can be an excellent way of easing students into the appropriate mood, or defining parameters that will help them identify the theme.

Yet while teachers find drama games useful and students obviously enjoy them, there's a danger that they can become a 'quick fix' — sufficient fun in themselves to distract students from the serious intentions of educational drama. Games can overexcite young children, and their pace often leads to a breakdown between cognitive and affective learning. For some students, drama signifies nothing more than games used as lesson breaks or fill-in activities before the bell. So this chapter takes a fresh look at drama games, and suggests a different perspective.

Comparing drama and games

There are four main similarities between drama and games:

- The need for rules
- Separation from the consequences of real life

- Tension
- Awareness of participants' roles.

These similarities provide the basis for using games as part of broader drama programming.

The need for rules

Drama and games both have a formal order: if the rules aren't followed, the game will break down or the drama will collapse (Bolton, 1987). Most games involve allocating different role functions to the players, who then interact according to set rules. For example, in *What's the Time, Mr Wolf?*, the wolf's role is to keep his back turned and only give chase after shouting "Dinner time!". Children demonstrate their awareness of the importance of rules by expressing outrage if rules are broken (e.g. if the wolf peeks). Yet, paradoxically, they will sometimes gleefully and deliberately flout the rules. For instance, they might call out the wrong formula question, the wolf might become 'Silly Old Kangaroo', or the object of the game might become not to escape the wolf but to get caught. Flouting usually leads to an alternative game of 'breaking the rules', where children branch off into a parody of the original.

The same sort of breakdown may happen in drama. Students can't create an alternative world unless they stay within an agreed paradigm. Nevertheless, they sometimes choose to flout it, satirising the original intention. For example, a play about outwitting the opposition might be disrupted by a child deliberately introducing a gun. There could be many reasons for this, but most probably in setting up the drama the teacher had been unable to engage the students' interest, or they didn't understand the 'rules'. Sometimes a class equates drama with excitement, and pulling a gun reminds them of TV or the movies. Generally speaking, however, games and drama both require the observation of rules, and are usually accompanied by a high degree of concentration or absorption.

Separation from the consequences of real life

Drama and games are both bracketed off from real life. It's possible to try out alternative actions with no external consequences. Thus, in a game of *Monopoly*, participants can gamble with money and property without any real loss; in a wartime drama, someone can play a traitor without really causing harm. This separation has been referred to as 'disinterested interest' — children are engaged in the action and care about what happens, but there's nothing permanent at stake.

Although drama requires a suspension of disbelief, students need to understand that even if they're operating within a fiction, they should be aware of the real world. The drama can collapse if they don't know what is real and what is not. If they ask questions like "Is this really happening?" or "Are you really a witch?", it indicates that the lines between reality and the drama world are becoming blurred. Sometimes drama roles can only be maintained if students have reality signalled to them very strongly. If you are working with students in the early years you may need to wear a hat or similar symbol to show that you're in role. It's also a good idea to allow young children to signal that they wish to escape the fiction if it cuts too close to their reality (e.g. "If you put your hands on your head and wear your invisible hat, you can't be seen by the witch").

Whenever you sense the need to break the fiction, you should have the class come out of role and reflect on what's happened in the drama. It may be best to come in and out of role several times, and it's especially important to spend time reflecting and de-roling after an emotionally strong episode. Questions like "When you were the hostage, how did you feel about ...?" can serve to re-establish reality.

These students have the freedom to 'try on' attitudes and dynamics that won't have lasting consequences when they step out of role.

THE REAL DEAL

What are 'real' consequences? For the purposes of this book, 'real' equates more or less with 'literal'. That is, the character of the wolf doesn't really eat those that s/he catches; the role is a fiction. Most sports would fall outside the definition of 'games' given here, simply because they have consequences that cannot be dismissed as notional, or suspended. If the soccer goalkeeper fails to stop the shot, a goal is literally scored!

Of course it's not easy to limit the consequences of games to the 'fiction' within which they're played. The fact is that games can have very real consequences for participants. Children can take the processes and the outcomes of games to heart, and they can affect relationships. As a teacher, you need to consider existing class dynamics when, for example, assigning roles. "Real" relationships of relative power and weakness, for example, should not be reinforced in games and drama activities simply because it seems 'natural' for students to take them up.

✷ Tension

Tension is generally present when conflicts or ambitions remain unresolved. This is as true of children's games as it is of adults' plays. For example, Hamlet can't obey his father's ghost and kill his uncle until he tests the ghost's validity, watches his uncle's reaction to the players re-enacting the murder, speaks with his mother, and so on. Tension sustains drama. When Hamlet does kill his uncle, the drama is all but over. The same sort of thing occurs in *Hide and Seek*, where the fun of the game is in the mounting tension as, one by one, the hidden players are found. As soon as all are caught, the game's over. According to Gavin Bolton (1984), teachers best inject tension into a drama by finding a way of preventing the climax. They can, for example, switch to slow motion, give secret instructions to some of the participants or release the ending and work in flashback. Thus the students can see the forces in conflict but the resolution is postponed or its importance diminished.

Awareness of participants' roles

Participants can only play a game if they understand what they're doing in relation to others. The hiders in a game of *Hide and Seek* must understand the intention of the seeker/s. If they don't, they're not likely to hide themselves effectively. Moreover, once they're caught, they're likely to reveal the locations of other hiders.

The same sort of thing happens in drama. To develop a role, it's essential to understand the roles and intentions of the other players. That's why students from different cultural contexts, or students learning English as an additional language, may need to be given a lot of information about the social or linguistic context of the drama and a clear idea of how people usually behave and speak in that situation.

Using drama games productively

When you're planning to use a drama game, you should be clear about your reasons for introducing it. It may be as a way of easing students from one way of thinking (e.g. individual, logical) into another (e.g. collaborative, lateral). It may be to focus their attention when they've just left the playground after recess. It may be a means of strategically mixing students — teaming them with classmates who are not part of their friendship groups. It is often used as a way of foreshadowing the theme of the ensuing drama. A game about convicts and overseers can be used to precede a drama which focuses on the colonial era.

Games are usually played at the beginning of a lesson, yet they may be more effective in the middle (to increase tension) or at the end (to help de-roling). What the game is, and where it's placed, will depend on the objective for the whole lesson.

Choosing the game

Many books (e.g. Moore, 1998; Matthews, 1988) include collections of games that can be adapted to drama. Games can be classified by the purpose they serve in a drama lesson, and in your planning it's important to make sure that there's a clear link between the game and the other phases of the lesson. Some key purposes for games are:

- fostering collaboration and trust
- building spatial awareness
- encouraging focused interactions around an emerging theme
- refocusing and reflecting after the drama.

FOSTERING COLLABORATION AND TRUST

Name games can set up a climate conducive to collaborative work, and they can be particularly useful when students don't know each other. Here are some common games, with suggestions for the next steps into drama.

1. Sitting in a circle, students call out their own names one by one. This beginning can be elaborated by adding an alliterative adjective to the name (e.g. "Happy Hannah"), and perhaps an illustrative action (e.g. jumping in the air with arms up). A drama about different feelings might start from grouping students with similar adjectives or actions.
2. Before giving their own names, students repeat the names of all the people in the circle ahead of them. This could be followed by a discussion about memory, and a drama based on remembering lists.
3. Students call out their names and add an item of food they bought at a shop — perhaps an alliterating item (e.g. "My name is Michael and I bought milk"). All of the items could then be combined as the only food left for a group abandoned on an island. (Don't reveal this before the game!)
4. Students add a rhythmic clicking of the fingers: two clicks before they call their names. This can be changed to clicking and calling the name of another person in the circle, who will then call someone else's (e.g. click-click "Hannah"; click-click "Yousuf"). The ensuing drama could use the tension this game creates to explore how people work under pressure.
5. If the students already know each other's names, they can choose a pseudonym (e.g. Gargantua) or a name they wish their parents had given them (e.g. Elvis). If the drama is to be based on a novel, they could choose the names of characters or role functions (e.g. "I'm Erica" or "I'm the grocer"), and this could become the basis for some improvisational work on incidents from the novel.

BUILDING SPATIAL AWARENESS

Movement games can make students comfortable with the spatial context for the drama and help mix the group. Here are a couple of examples.

The sun shines on

Students sit on chairs in a circle while you stand in the centre. You identify some visible feature or object that some of the students share (e.g. "The sun shines on all people … with curly hair / wearing a watch / in sneakers"). Those who fit the category must stand and change chairs with someone else. This can be done slowly until the game has been learned; then you join in, sitting on a chair, so that each round ends with a student in the centre to choose the next category. You can allow yourself to be 'caught' if you want to re-establish control of the category-naming. You might also stop the game when you see that students are sitting apart from their usual partners, or when the boys are mixed with the girls. You can vary things by speeding up the pace or allowing non-visible categories (e.g. "all people who … own pets / have brothers"). The ensuing drama could use pairs or triads of the newly mixed students.

Tag

One student is 'It' and hunts the others, who can be saved only by grouping in the numbers you call out (e.g. threes). Once caught, students join the hunter in catching the others, leading into an 'us or them' drama.

A less physical but noisier tag involves students closing their eyes and listening for sounds (e.g. animal calls) that identify like characters for them to join. This could be the basis of a drama where different animal groups debate the use of a forest area.

ENCOURAGING FOCUSED INTERACTIONS

Too often, drama can remain at the level of a series of games. For cognitive and affective learning, the drama needs to focus on the exploration of a chosen theme or issue. The game needs to ease into this theme.

Working with a partner or small group in a game can be the first step into a gradually deepening drama.

Mirrors

With partners sitting on the floor facing each other, B becomes the image of A in the mirror. A moves one or both hands, slowly and silently, allowing B to reflect the movements simultaneously. You freeze the movement and B takes over the lead. When this game works, the partners anticipate each other's actions, holding muscles slightly tense to correct any wrong guesses about the next move.

To ease into a theme you can specify the action to be mirrored — an inexperienced cook preparing a meal, a woman dressing for dinner, a clown putting on make-up — and the mirroring thus becomes the first step in a drama about a dinner party or a circus. The mirror game can also be used at the mid-point of a lesson to help students further into the drama, or at the end to help them de-role.

Mirroring talk

Two lines, As and Bs, face each other. The As describe their morning slowly and clearly to the Bs, who attempt to speak along with them by anticipating their words and watching their mouths as they speak. At intervals you freeze the talk and the B line moves along so that each 'B' student faces a new partner. The As continue their original stories with their new partner, who gradually accumulate a range of fractured stories. Any combination of the stories can become the theme of a drama.

Master–Servant

A and B take it in turns to issue and obey orders (e.g. "Sit, fold your arms and hum"). You may need to emphasise that orders should not be humiliating to the partner. A variation is for one of the partners to be blindfolded and safely guided, by word or touch, around the room. The drama which follows could explore themes related to status and the need for trust.

Story-telling with objects

A gives an object to B, who is blindfolded, and asks questions that lead B to construct a story around the object (e.g. "What does this feel like? What does it remind you of? What character does it suggest to you? What are they wearing?" and so on). Then the roles are reversed, B leading A with a different object. The characters created in these stories can develop an improvised scene to begin a drama.

Improvising with objects

A and B share an object, which becomes something found at a sale. Each must attempt to argue (politely) why they need it. At the end of the game, some of the discussions can be pooled to become the basis of a drama, for example, about the commercialisation of Christmas.

Students can develop lateral thinking with a game where objects passed around the circle are used in imaginative ways (e.g. a tambour becomes an earring or a mirror, a glue stick becomes a torch). Some of these objects could then be linked into a drama about a magical world where nothing is as it seems.

REFOCUSING AND REFLECTING

Games are not only used as a way into drama. As shown in the examples below, they can be introduced during a drama for pausing and refocusing, or at the end to consolidate the experience.

Grandma's footsteps

Also known as Red Light, Green Light, this can be adapted to refocus attention on an emerging theme. One person — the watcher — stands at one end of the room, back turned. The group attempts to sneak up on the watcher, who suddenly turns. Anyone caught moving is 'out'. In a drama about landing on an alien planet, this game might be introduced after several scenes (e.g. choosing the crew, near-mutiny, landing) as a way of slowing the action and focusing on the need for caution. The watcher serves as guard of the spaceship and the rest of the group become natives of the planet Jupiter. The number of guards can be increased if you want the Earthling not to be overwhelmed.

Find the hands

Partners face each other and get to know each other's hands by touch. Then, blindfolded or keeping eyes closed, they join a larger group and explore hands until the partner is found.

This game can be placed at the end of a drama where differences have been resolved — perhaps different tribes at peace with each other or family members reconciled. It serves to cement the feeling of 'togetherness' and leads easily into de-roling and a discussion of the affective learning.

References and sources

Bolton, G (1987) 'Drama as Art.' Paper presented at the British Council course 'How Do You Train a Drama Leader?', Durham, UK.

Bolton, G (1984). *Drama as Education*. Longman, London.

Matthews, S (1988) *Getting into the Act*. GP Books, New Zealand.

Moore, P (1988) *When Are We Going to Have More Drama?*. Nelson, Sydney.

CHAPTER THREE

Getting into it:
Movement, mime and still image

Concentrating on different ways of moving the body is often a useful way of beginning drama with primary-age children. Enactment is at the heart of drama, and a major part of enactment is using the body to express attitudes and ways of feeling and thinking. Observing and exploring the meanings generated by bodies moving in space can ease children into other modes of drama.

Creating meaning through movement, mime and still image helps to develop skills in concentration and observation. Working without words can be more manageable for young and inexperienced students — it's a more tangible way of expressing what they've observed about the world. It's also a good method of helping new arrivals in the country, or new speakers of English, to bridge cultural boundaries.

Although some movement is instinctive and intuitive, living in a particular culture teaches people to use their bodies in particular ways. Cultural practices can imprint themselves in ways that reveal differences in:

- the acceptable level of directness
- the customary level of expressiveness
- the types of gestures customarily used
- what certain gestures signify
- customary physical proximity/intimacy.

All of this means that students have much to explore, and to communicate to one another, about the relationship between movement and meaning. It also means that you may have to think twice about movements that you might initially consider 'natural' or universal.

Relaxation exercises

Relaxation exercises can provide a useful beginning (and ending) for movement activities because they help students put aside other issues and become more aware of their bodies. They also break the inertia of sitting-at-table activities. Those of you who haven't used relaxation exercises before can be assured that the following procedures are 'tried and true' starting points. Further ideas are to be found in Steve Matthews' *Getting into the Act* (1988).

1. Ask students to find a clear space on the floor. Insist that there's to be no talking. Play some relaxing music and ask them to take deep breaths to the count of four, and then hold for four before exhaling. Nominate individual parts of the body, beginning with the toes or head and moving to the other extremity. Suggest that the students consciously tense each body part in succession and then allow it to become 'heavy' and relaxed.

2. If there's not enough space for all the students to lie, begin with stretching exercises. Again stipulate that students shouldn't touch each other. Suggest that they imagine they are stretching with all their might towards the ceiling to touch something that's just out of reach. Then nominate each body part in isolation (again moving from one end of the body to the other) and demonstrate the actions as you suggest them. For example: "Your head's all floppy. Move it gently from side to side, then around in a circle — first one way, then the other. Now turn your head to the right, pretending that you're trying to hear your sister's conversation through the wall. Now do the same to the left."

Movement

In order to become more aware of how actions convey meanings, we need to understand how our bodies are located, both in the space immediately surrounding us and in the larger space shared by the group. Students can develop their awareness of space by exploring their own personal space. They can, for example, move around the room carrying their space as an imaginary capsule, taking care not to bump or intrude on anyone else's capsule. They can think about how closely they stand when talking with friends, and contrast this with the distance they keep when speaking to people they don't really know or with whom they feel less confident. In time they'll come to realise that different people require different amounts of space, and that an invasion of personal space can appear threatening.

Moving around the room making use of high, middle and lower levels can help students become aware of the infinite ways bodies are used to communicate ideas, emotions or events. Often this is unintentional. To highlight this, you may initially need to provide movement suggestions for the whole class. Students can think of themselves as a silk scarf fluttering to the ground, a piece of wallpaper slowly peeling from the wall, or a dob of margarine or butter simmering in a frying pan. They can be encouraged to use every level of their space, side to side as well as up and down. Mirror activities in pairs can help them explore all the space in front of them, just as choosing three different spots in the room and moving to each in turn can help them expand their use of available space.

Rhythm and tempo have an impact on how we make meaning. For example, a fast pace may indicate excitement. Percussion instruments are useful for establishing rhythm and tempo. Tambourines and drums produce a variety of sounds which can spark students' imaginations and help them to vary the pace at which they move. Tapes of a variety of music (e.g. Handel's *Water Music*, Vivaldi's *Four Seasons* and Grof's *Grand Canyon Suite*) are handy to have to create a desired mood.

Mime

Mime is a more disciplined, exaggerated form of movement with the specific intention of conveying meaning to an outside observer. While this ancient medium of artistic expression has had many definitions, it's best understood as the use of the body to explore or communicate an idea, concept, emotion or story. Usually it's performed wordlessly. Some purists insist on complete silence, eliminating any music or sound effects, but in the classroom it's sufficient for meaning to be concentrated mostly in chosen movements of the body.

In order to set up a mime, students need to look closely at the physical world, to observe others carefully and to become more aware of how they communicate nonverbally. It gives opportunities for representing actions or emotions precisely and imaginatively, with the stress either on exploring or communicating them.

When you're preparing for mime activities, you may find it helpful to begin with the sort of isolation and relaxation exercises mentioned earlier, so that students can develop their awareness and control of different parts of their bodies. There are other activities, too, that may help them to change gear and focus on the coming drama. For example, they can be asked to:

- walk around the room, moving as if they were feeling happy/angry/shy/proud
- convey an urgent message (e.g. *Quick, come over here!*), first with hands only, then with feet, and finally with whole bodies
- in pairs, give and receive a gift, conveying what it is through the giver's actions and gestures and the receiver's response
- mould an imaginary lump of clay into a recognisable object through mimed action around the class circle
- pass a nominated imaginary object (e.g. a hot plate, a wet rag, a handful of limp spaghetti) around the class circle.

A young or inexperienced class may find it easier to begin miming activities as a whole group. You can lead them by narrating a story while the whole class mimes actions, events or feelings as the story unfolds. A variation on this is what Peter Slade (1973:30) has called "the ideas game", in which students suggest three things for the teacher to link into a narrative. Usually one will involve movement and the use of space: for example, the students might offer 'hat', 'bicycle' and 'Christmas Day', which you can link into an improvised narrative about a family celebration. The story told should have some connection with the focus of the lesson. If you were looking at the concept of homelessness after war, for instance, you might begin your story like this:

> We are very cold and tired because we've been walking all day. We've been walking across fields covered in snow. The wind is bitter and blowing in our faces, and it's becoming very hard to keep going. But we know that if we stop we'll get even colder. We're so wet that our bodies are very heavy. Our legs feel as if they're made of lead …

Later, you might use percussion instruments to develop a tense moment, highlight a pause or represent the mood being conveyed.

With mime in the classroom, the emphasis is on detail and accuracy in depiction rather than on artistry and technique. Successful mime requires both actors and audience to suspend their disbelief and accept the illusion being created. When someone mimes lifting a large, heavy box, for example, the audience must feel that it's large and heavy because of the position of the body, the outstretched arms and the facial exertion. To mime eating a ripe mango means evoking the sensations of its taste, smell and slippery flesh purely through movement and gesture.

Mask and mime

You may sometimes wish to increase the power of communication by combining mime with the use of a mask. Putting on a mask can be symbolic of stepping out of one's own self to take on another role. Students who are reluctant to try mime can find a mask liberating. Simple masks can be made from paper plates or material and elastic. Even the ubiquitous red clown nose or face paint will serve as an initial form of mask. Neutral or universal masks are easy to make from plaster bandages, and can represent countless characters. They illustrate particularly well how the body can be used to convey ideas and emotions that are usually conveyed facially.

Still image

Alongside movement, stillness can also be explored as a method of embodying and communicating meaning. The technique of still image can be a valuable introductory drama strategy. It involves students in using their bodies to create an image (sometimes called a frozen moment, depiction or tableau) that represents how a selected moment or incident might look. Just as photos are taken to record particular instants and occasions, or the pause button on the video is pressed to examine a significant frame for a bit longer, so still images allow attitudes and feelings to be captured at one point in time. Observing an image can lead to discussion and further reflection — even a second image.

One way of creating a still image is for some students to become 'sculptors', using the bodies of other students as 'thinking clay' to shape their interpretation of a significant moment. For example, a student might sculpt the final scene in *The Paper Bag Princess* (Munsch, 1989), using three classmates to depict Ronald, Elizabeth and the exhausted dragon. He or she would need to find a way to demonstrate Ronald's disgust at Elizabeth's appearance, and Elizabeth's contemptuous response. The two parents and two children in Anthony Browne's *Voices in the Park* (1998) also provide excellent starting points for sculpting. Students being sculpted allow themselves to be directed by the sculptor, although they may need to check that they are accurately representing the sculptor's intentions. Ironically, the process of creating the silent still image involves a challenging use of directed language and active listening.

Still images can also be made by small groups shaping themselves into a representation of a significant moment or emotion. Members can take turns to step out of the group and give directions, or one can act as 'director'. Groups can equally well choose a sequence of significant moments from a story to present as a series of freeze frames. However, it's important to discuss the reasons behind their choice of moments; it's often through such discussions that learning becomes clear.

Working on still image in a small group helps students to translate thoughts, ideas or critical incidents into a tangible form that can be discussed and, if necessary, remade. Similarly, a group can work together to create an abstract, or a more complex, concept. The image at left resulted from a discussion of the phrase 'turning a blind eye'.

The focus is on group interpretation rather than on individual effort, and this development of joint enterprise is essential to fostering any co-operative work in the classroom.

Once presented, still images can be 'unfrozen' and animated for a few moments of improvisation, movement or mime. Alternatively, you or another student may simply 'tap in' to each character's thoughts or feelings by lightly touching each one on the shoulder. If the characters are limited to one or two words in response, they have to focus on communicating through movement.

Still image can also be used to explore real issues that students are facing at school. They might be asked, for example, to present an image of a conflict they've recently experienced. Fiction texts might provide the starting point for explorations like these. For example, one teacher chose the picture book *Willy and Hugh* (Browne, 1991) as a starting point for exploring issues of friendship with a Year 1 class. First she asked her students to use their bodies to show how Willy was feeling at the beginning of the story (i.e. rejected, alone) and to contrast this with how he felt after making friends with Hugh (more self-confident, happier). In a subsequent lesson, they sculpted each other to portray these feelings. Finally, before the ending of the text was shared, they were asked to create a freeze frame that might conclude the story.

The same approach can be taken in presenting and discussing images of issues in which students are not so directly involved, such as euthanasia, pollution, land rights or drug addiction. Not only will their awareness of such critical issues be heightened, they will appreciate that there are always a number of perspectives to be considered before judgements are made.

References and sources

Browne, A (1998) *Voices in the Park*. Doubleday, London.

Browne, A (1991) *Willy and Hugh*. Julia MacRae, London.

Matthews, S (1988) *Getting into the Act*. GP Books, New Zealand.

Munsch, R (1989) *The Paper Bag Princess*. Ashton Scholastic, Sydney.

Slade, P (1973) *Child Drama*. University of London Press, London.

Happy
?retty
                    I will Loo
                     after y
                while   is
                    your mo

endry

Lovely

Linde

CHAPTER FOUR

Exploring teacher in role and mantle of the expert

Teacher in role and *mantle of the expert* are drama techniques that derive from the work of Dorothy Heathcote in the 1960s and which have been continually developed and reconceptualised to produce approaches such as 'leaderly drama' (Hasemen, 2001) and enactment of the expert (Hughes, 2001). Regular use of these techniques can change the dynamics of your classroom, offering your students more control over both the content and direction of the drama and the learning process. They enable students to walk in someone else's shoes and at the same time confirm the importance of their own understandings and experiences. Yet though both strategies are useful right across the learning areas, they remain under-used in primary classrooms. This chapter aims to demonstrate their application and value.

Teacher in role

Why use teacher in role?
When Dorothy Heathcote first developed teacher in role in the 1960s, it was a controversial technique. The orthodoxy of the time held that child-centred, 'progressive' teaching should allow children's creativity to flower with little interference by the teacher. Gavin Bolton (1984), reflecting on his early contact with teacher in role, wrote:

> Like many others I resisted its usage at first, not because it was not effective, but because the idea of a teacher actually 'joining in' was more than my traditional teacher training and attitude to professionalism could stomach (p 8).

'Child-centredness' has never meant restricting learning to what the child already knows. After all, unless you promote more than the status quo, there is little point in your lesson. Once Heathcote's technique was properly understood, it became clear that although the teacher took on a role and entered the drama world, s/he could unobtrusively ensure students' centrality in the work, particularly if the adopted role was low in status. Heathcote herself believed that it was the teacher's responsibility to "be able to 'forward' the work towards teaching ends without destroying the children's contribution" (Bolton, 1984:52).

The benefit of teaching in role is that you can act less as a direct teller and more as an indirect informer. For example, you can use your voice in such a way that you're giving information while apparently asking for it. You might say: "I've heard they're limiting our water use. Why would they do that just when we need it most?" In other words, you can organise your students' learning from inside the drama world, using your adopted character for subtle pointing — or more forceful emphasis — when significant issues arise.

Teacher in role is particularly aimed at developing metacognition. Heathcote observed that her aim was to

> ... show them the implications of what they are doing. I must create reflective participation. If I don't do that, I'm not in art of any kind and I'm not in learning. Also I want to show that in any situation there's a mesh of interests ... You can best consider big themes by narrowing the situation right down (in Robinson, 1980:27–28).

The importance of careful planning

Although teacher in role involves a high degree of spontaneity, it also requires meticulously planned scaffolding. Haseman (2001) highlights the crucial role of anticipating themes that may emerge, drama strategies that could be employed and resources that could be needed. Potential resources are organised and ready but are not produced unless called for in the drama that eventuates. In a well-equipped primary classroom, many of these resources are already on hand, e.g. the dress-up box, paper and textas, musical instruments, records and maps.

Before beginning a lesson in role, you need to test students' level of interest in a particular topic or idea, or plan how to engage this interest. You also need to think about how to elicit what the students already know, how to challenge some of their preconceptions, how to extend their knowledge of content, and how to encourage them to reflect on what they've experienced.

Steps in planning

1. Finding themes and identifying learning goals

The first step is to decide on a broad **content area** and a range of possible **outcomes**. For example, the class may start with a broad theme or topic in Studies in Society, such as refugees. As the students' understanding and interests are revealed, you might narrow the theme, perhaps by pursuing an understanding of displacement. Chapter 10 provides a sample unit demonstrating how a theme like this might be explored in a group containing a number of ESL learners.

Choosing an issue that features in a district newspaper will ensure its relevance to the students. This may be a very local issue — such as the threatened loss of a netball court — or a broader issue with local ramifications, such as groundwater salinity.

It's important to motivate students by choosing an attractive lure into the drama. Students can be engaged by a photograph — perhaps one of Neil Armstrong walking on the moon — linked to a provocative question, such as: "I wonder if everyday problems are more or less important when you're a long way from home?".

As students develop greater familiarity and independence, you can open the planning process up to them. The lesson plan itself becomes a fully shared experience, with your students suggesting not only themes but episodes that might be explored.

2. Adding depth

Having decided with the class on the theme or topic, you need to consider the deeper meaning or metaphor it might represent — the wider application it may have. By deliberately working in layers of meaning, you can begin to establish an aesthetic dimension to the work. The topic of refugees, for example, could be linked to the idea of 'security' at a number of levels: *physical* security for homeless people seeking refuge; *national* security (in both the host nation and the nation of origin); and *emotional* security among people in the host nation and among those seeking refuge.

3. Adopting roles

Next, you need to consider suitable roles for the class and yourself. Be careful to offer students roles that are interesting in themselves. It's usual to begin with a category of role (e.g. detectives, astronauts, farmers) that students can individualise as they wish. You can also suggest more specific roles for individuals by saying things like: "Is the farmer who specialises in growing rice here?". Allowing students to choose their roles will strengthen their enactment because it allows for deeper engagement with the content.

The role and status you adopt depend on what you see as the best way to facilitate the drama. A high-status role (e.g. Minister for Primary Industries) may not challenge the class sufficiently because it doesn't position students in a relationship to you that is very different from the usual one. On the other hand, a low-status role may be inappropriate with a new class, when teacher–student dynamics are being established. A good middle ground in this case is a 'second-in-charge' role, in which you can't take final decisions but have to consult with your boss (who might be absent). Thus you can introduce delays, perhaps presenting yourself to the class as a character sympathetic to their aims. For example, in a role-play where the students are vets wanting to inspect a zoo for mistreated animals, you might be the person in charge of the lions, who has to defer to the head keeper and asks for time to consult. Nonetheless, if you're working with an early-years class, you would typically adopt a very low status — 'the one who doesn't know', like the work-experience student who's come for advice about caring for animals.

4. Setting expectations

When first introducing teacher in role, you should be specific about what the students can expect. You might say: "When I put on this hat [or scarf or spectacles], I'm not going to be me; I'm going to be someone different. Can you tell from what I say and do who I am?" Using the prop as a signal for coming in and out of role, you can interrupt the drama with narrative links to shift backwards and forwards in time. Sometimes, too, you'll see a need to come out of role to reflect on what's happening, or to get the class to decide — out of role and objectively weighing alternative possibilities — what to do in the next episode.

5. Setting the scene

It's crucial to prepare your introductory in-role address to the class. What you say should induct them into the 'game', letting them know who you are, who they are, what the context is and why you are meeting. As they gain experience, your introduction can be more indirect. For example, you might open by saying:

> **Thank you for coming to the upper deck. I wanted to find a space where the passengers won't hear us, and I think it's safe to say that they're all in the dining room now.**

By now the students should have picked up that they are on some sort of ship (after all, it has a deck and passengers). It should also be clear that they aren't passengers themselves, even though they don't yet know exactly who they are. They might guess that they are the crew and that you are the captain, but before they can enter the drama world confidently, they need a few more clues:

> **The captain has given me full authority to act for him. He doesn't want to alarm the passengers by leaving the dining room. You may have wondered why, when you signed on to crew for this mission, we made sure that you'd had at least some medical training. I'm afraid I have bad news: this spaceship shows evidence that the virus has come on board.**

Now the students have a setting and a range of possible roles, and they know that you're only the second-in-command, not the one with ultimate control.

For teacher in role to work, all of the students have to be playing the same game — in other words, contributing to the focus that you set. If students 'pull focus' — have a heart attack, or create an alternative tension (e.g. by inventing an imminent invasion by aliens) — the drama may not work, and the rules of the game may need to be spelt out more clearly.

6. Giving direction

Because they are used to stories and the story genre, younger students can become preoccupied with 'what happens next' rather than 'why this is so'. Your drama may be more effective if you 'give away' or jointly predetermine the ending. That way, the students can concentrate on what's happening now.

7. Developing character

If you're working with early-years students, you might invite them to help you embody your role. For example: "I want to act as a witch, but I'm not sure how I would walk or talk". Students can demonstrate both: they might stand with a crooked back, and speak in a high, shrill voice. They might even sculpt your body. In that way, it becomes clear to them that the drama is really pretence.

Some features of teacher in role

Teacher in role is a complex game of improvisation, involving 'offers' by both teacher and students. Part of the skill of teaching in role is being able to recognise and support a student offer that has real potential for deepening exploration of the theme, and correspondingly to deflect attention from irrelevant offerings.>
Thus, in the spaceship drama sketched above, a student might promote a clearer definition of the impending disaster by saying: "This virus mightn't be fatal. Have you done any tests to work out what it is?". However, a student who says "I'm not a doctor; I'm one of the passengers" hasn't cued into the introduction. It might be a good time for you to come out of role and clarify the implications of taking such a stance.

> This skill is explored in detail in the PETA publication On Task: Focused Literacy Learning (Edwards-Groves, 2003).

Teacher in role is especially useful for exploring common, or universal, qualities among people who otherwise appear dissimilar. For example, by adopting the role of medico-astronauts on the virus-infected spaceship, the students are joined in fellowship with all people who wish to protect others from information that may hurt them. This fellowship doesn't hold truth or certainty, though. The notion of withholding information for someone else's good simply becomes a universal 'holding area' for a range of interpretations (Simons, 1997). In role, your aim is to explore the 'holding area' precisely because it can be interpreted differently by different people. In *their* roles, the students' different ways of seeing and understanding are bound to contest the orthodox logic of any fellowship.

Mantle of the expert

The corollary of low-status or 'inexpert' teacher in role is high-status or expert student in role. In this technique, a group of students act as experts in some enterprise (e.g. as historians or farm managers). It is important that the other participants respect their claim to expertise as they go about solving the problems that they've been consulted about. The students are not merely *told* that they are experts, their authority is established over time through drama work in which their status is created and enacted. Fleming (1994:100) suggests that "a group who will eventually advise on bullying may first establish their expertise as education experts by advising on the best height for school chairs, the appropriate range of colours for school crayons, or how to change a classroom to accommodate a blind pupil".

The validity of statements by the 'expert' students shouldn't be questioned during the drama: they are, after all, operating in a fictional world, and their status may collapse if they're challenged on minor mistakes. Thus, in a drama about an alligator, an expert zoologist who says that kangaroos come from Africa won't forfeit respect, since the claim doesn't affect the body of the drama. The true fact can be established later, if necessary, during a reflection period. In fact, it's often while students are in role that they're motivated to learn about a particular area or skill. Thus students in role as convicts transported to Australia might research details of a particular penal settlement in order to plan an escape. You could enter the drama as a newly arrived convict unaware of the escape plan, becoming again 'the one who doesn't know'.

References and sources

Bolton, G (1984) *Drama as Education*. Longman, London.

Burton, B (1991) *The Act of Learning*. Longman Cheshire, Melbourne.

Edwards-Groves, C (2003) *On Task: Focused Literacy Learning*. Primary English Teaching Association, Sydney.

Fleming, M (1994) *Starting Drama Teaching*. David Fulton, London.

Haseman, (2001) 'The Leaderly Process. Drama and the Artistry of 'Rip, Mix & Burn". In Rasmussen, B & Ostern, A, *Playing Betwixt & Between: The IDEA Dialogues*. IDEA Publications, Bergen/Straume.

Hughes, J (2000) 'Drama as a Learning Medium: Researching Poetry'. *The Primary Educator* 6 (3).

Simons, J (1997) "Universalising' Ambiguity & Difference'. Keynote for Council of Ontario Drama Educators. Niagara on the Lake, Canada.

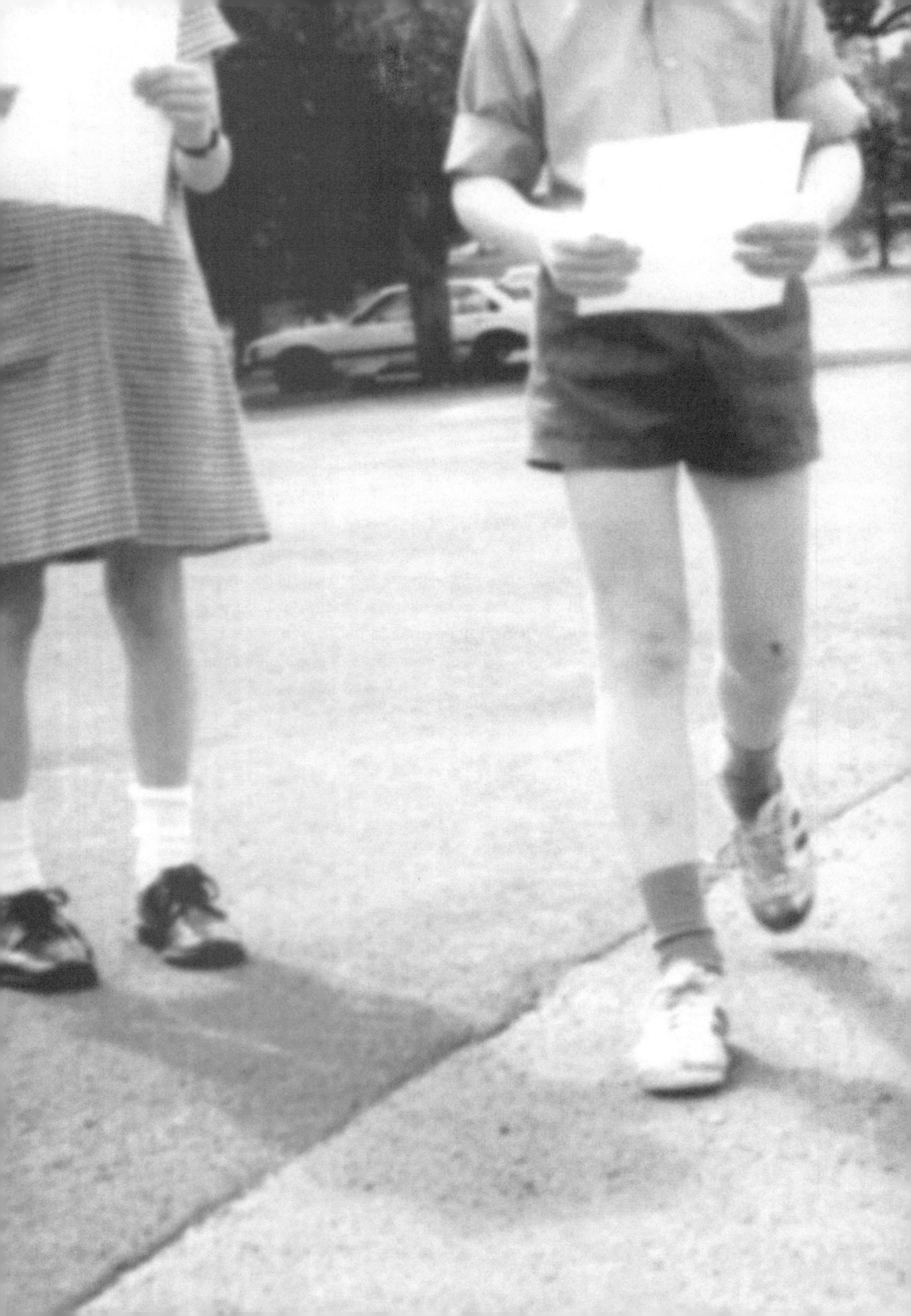

CHAPTER FIVE

Programming using drama strategies and literary texts

This chapter focuses on programming teaching and learning in drama, considering drama both as one of the creative arts and as a strategy that can be used across the curriculum. While literature and literacy provide starting points for some of the examples included, any learning area can be used as a beginning, and the approach can be either subject-based or integrated.

More than ever, educators are adopting models of curriculum organisation and planning that enable them to make as many meaningful linkages across disciplines as possible (see, for example, PETA's *Practical Literacy Programming* (2002)). In this aim, the power and versatility of drama is particularly valuable. Further, drama has unique possibilities for helping students to change concepts, attitudes or beliefs that are part of their 'saturated consciousness' (Apple, 1990) and which remain unquestioned.

Drama makes it much easier to examine critically issues like gender and social status. From their first year at school, students can explore issues such as equity, co-operation and oppression through depicting the sleepy, weepy, overworked duck or the lazy old farmer in *Farmer Duck* (Waddell & Oxenbury, 1991). Several drama techniques can be useful in exploring how and why the farmer came to be so tired and lazy, and what kind of plan the rest of the animals formulated to save the duck. These include depiction, tapping in and hot-seating.

Before looking at some examples in depth, this chapter will consider how outcomes-based planning affects the teaching of drama.

Outcomes and drama

In Australia, outcomes-based education has presented programming difficulties in all the creative arts. This is not because of any intrinsic problem with an approach based on outcomes. Rather, it is because outcomes have tended to be interpreted in a *technical* sense — as behaviours that students will be able to demonstrate at the end of a lesson or unit of work.

This was never the sole intention of the approach. Bill Spady (1992), one of those responsible for introducing the notion of outcomes-based education to Australia, suggested that educators wouldn't get very far in preparing people for the demands of the twenty-first century unless they started looking at the 'big picture' by addressing life-changing or *transformational* outcomes.

For example, what do you really hope the students in your class will achieve by being in your class? What do you want them to take with them at the end of the year — or, even bigger, at the end of Year 6/7 or Year 12?

It's impossible to confine drama outcomes to the technical kind. You can't always observe what sort of learning has taken place at the end of a lesson, or even after a series of lessons. New understandings may be realised over time — sometimes months or years later— and changes in attitudes, values and beliefs are not always easy to measure. You won't necessarily be able to demonstrate that you have achieved the particular outcomes you have planned. However, that shouldn't prevent you from thinking about long-term purposes, as well as what you expect to happen as a result of a number of lessons.

The arts enable you to consider the way students learn in a way that other disciplines don't. For example, you can look much more at *process* than content when using drama across the curriculum. Drama can effect change because it puts the learner at the centre of the learning process in a way that is quite different from more traditional and technical approaches to teaching and learning, which are more teacher-centred.

Drama techniques enable you to establish the deep understanding, quality learning environments and meaningful learning contexts discussed in recent documents about teaching and learning (e.g. NSW DET, 2003; Education Queensland, 2001). In addition, the drama process enables students to develop generic competencies — things like solving problems, taking risks and communicating effectively. That being the case, you needn't feel too concerned if drama teaching doesn't fit the parameters of more technical ways of teaching and learning.

Bringing about change

Jonathan Neelands (1990) suggests that the overall purpose in programming for drama is to bring about change. It might be change in level of understanding, attitude, expectation, social behaviour, use of language, or awareness of others and their particular needs. Some experience or trigger — which might well come up in another learning area — will generally prompt your decision to look at a particular theme or issue through the medium of drama. The students will be 'framed' in terms of some dramatic convention or form (e.g. still image, readers' theatre, teacher in role or mime). They may be framed as narrators, reporters/researchers, or perhaps as onlookers, and this will lead to the selection of a particular focus. Over time, after opportunities to work through the issues in dramatic form, you and the students will reflect on particular things that have emerged.

The overall plan must, of course, be broken down into reasonable expectations for the year, the term, the unit of work and, eventually, a specific lesson. Each lesson must be seen as part of a coherent sequence that builds towards your outcomes and focus.

Indeed, one of the most important things in teaching drama is to provide time at appropriate moments for debriefing — getting out of role and reflecting on the whole experience. This can be as simple as asking students to talk about how they felt when they were in role. Younger students can be asked to step out of the imaginary role physically, or turn around or shake their body parts to 'shake the drama out'.

TEN STEPS IN PLANNING

In order to program for Drama work you should consider:

1. Who are the learners? Consider the age and experience of your students, and the way that they relate to each other and to you. What sort of action will you need to take to help them adopt and stay in role, and observe the principles of good behaviour?

2. Who are you? What sort of drama do you feel most comfortable with, and how can you extend your own range? What will help *you* to take risks? (Usually this will involve anticipating what could happen, and planning a range of contingent responses.)

3. Where is the drama work coming from? Is it intended as an Arts experience, or is it a technique for exploring a topic which arises in another learning area?

4. What are your intended outcomes? These should be connected with outcomes in Drama or the other learning areas. For example, you may wish to promote an effective use of mime to convey emotions or use hot-seating to examine the effects of mining the Antarctic.

5. What is the fiction to be explored? You will need to choose a metaphor; for example, the students may adopt the roles of 'sad clowns' who are forced to be funny. You may want them to think about the differences between appearance and reality.

6. What sort of drama devices/techniques will you plan for the students to use? If you are playbuilding, you will need to consider a range of possible devices.

7. What sort of resources can you provide to help motivate or extend the drama?

8. What will be your teaching technique? Will you be inside the drama, as a teacher in role? Will you be side coaching, partially in it, or external to the drama, giving instructions or negotiating ideas? Perhaps you will need to switch between these.

9. How much time should you spend on each section of the lesson? Don't take too long on games or other introductory steps; allow enough time for negotiation and discussion. How will you de-role the students?

10. How will you evaluate the teaching/learning? What you do needs to be related to your targeted outcomes.

Starting with literature

This section sets out several sample drama sequences for students working at different stages across the primary school, using devices described in previous chapters.

FARMER DUCK

Suitability   Years K–2
Duration   Six sessions of 20–25 minutes each

Anticipated outcomes

Students will develop the ability to:

- use gesture and facial expression to demonstrate understanding and interpretation of a story
- provide verbal and nonverbal responses to questions
- recognise that words on a page have meaning and can be read aloud
- engage in role and represent ideas through the body
- understand the different phases of a story: orientation, complication, resolution
- work co-operatively in a small group.

Focus

A co-operative working environment. Respect for others' contributions.

Learning experiences

Session 1 Read the text together. Study the pictures and discuss the story. In a rereading, encourage the students to interact using animal voices. Draw students' attention to how they can vary the intonation of the animal noises to indicate how the animal is feeling.

Session 2 Reread the text. Ask students to select their favourite animal and individually depict it (e.g. a tired duck, a helpful cow, a lazy farmer) with their bodies. Alternatively, students can sculpt a partner. Discuss how our bodies reflect how we are feeling. Students can then depict their animal in a contrasting frame of mind (e.g. a happy, energetic duck).

Session 3 Ask students, in groups of three, to 'read' the words of a particular character as the text is revisited. Discuss how a change in tone of voice can express feelings, e.g. degrees of tiredness, laziness, anxiety or depression. Use the example of the duck becoming more depressed and exhausted as the story unfolds.

Session 4 Ask small groups (3–4) of students to depict a moment from the beginning, middle or end of the story. Each group presents its moment and the rest of the class 'reads' the scene depicted. 'Tap in' at various points to hear how a particular character is feeling.

Session 5 In order to establish the difference between thought and speech, have students complete a worksheet where they replace the duck's "Quack!" with an English equivalent in a thought bubble. Students share their 'scripts' with the class.

Session 6 Prepare a simple readers' theatre script. Divide students into groups of five (ducks, cows, hens, sheep and farmers) to read their parts in collaboration with you as narrator.

To conclude: Ask students to illustrate what sessions they liked or disliked (see a Kindergarten/Reception student's example below).

THE WEREWOLF KNIGHT

Suitability   Years 3–4
Duration   Nine sessions of 40–45 minutes each

Anticipated outcomes

Students will continue to develop:
- knowledge about the characteristic patterns of different texts (e.g. fairy tales)
- co-operative skills
- the ability to use language effectively for different social purposes
- the ability to question texts rather than accept the surface meaning.

Focus

Going beyond stereotypes and prejudgements. Not judging a book by its cover.

Learning experiences

Session 1 Explore the students' preconceived notions of werewolves and knights. Ask students individually to list the images/concepts that they associate with werewolves and knights. Build up databases about werewolves and knights on the board. Compare the databases.

Session 2 Have students select one word or phrase from each database to speak expressively as a werewolf (e.g. 'hiss', 'snarl', 'sharp teeth') or as a knight (e.g. 'shining armour', 'brave rescue', 'noble ideals'). These are co-operatively choreographed as a soundscape. Add percussion instruments if desired.

Discuss the implicit tension between someone who is both a werewolf and a knight.

Session 3 Read the first page:

> Feolf was a knight and a good friend of the king, but at other times he was a werewolf. When the moon rose over the fir trees, Sir Feolf slipped away to the forest, hid his clothes under a rock and turned into a wolf. All night long he ran in the forest, enjoying his dark and wolfish things; then when dawn came he turned into a man and went home. And no one was any the wiser.

Ask pairs of students to take turns sculpting each other as werewolves and knights. Those sculpted as werewolves become a 'museum' of statues while the other half observes. This action is repeated with the knights. Werewolves and knights then stand back to back and, to the count of ten, slowly change into their alterego — and then back again.

As a group, observe differences and similarities between each representation. Discuss what expectations students have of fairy tales such as this one. How do they expect things to end? What characteristics do knights/princesses/kings usually have?

Session 4 Read the next two pages, which end with Fioran's fear that Feolf no longer loves her. Set up two lines of students as a 'conscience alley'. A student in role as Feolf walks down the middle as each student, in role as a member of the court, loudly offers advice about whether or not to tell Fioran he is a werewolf. After listening to the advice offered, each student writes in role as Feolf about why he will or will not tell Fioran he is a werewolf.

Session 5 Panel hot-seat Fioran's best friend, the palace gossip and Feolf's valet about their reactions to Feolf's confession. If students have not participated in hot-seating, you could first ask them to list questions that they would like to ask.

Read the next page, where Fioran seeks the magician's advice.

Session 6 Ask students to predict what might happen now that a complication has been introduced. They can present orientation and complication fragments of the story as frozen moments and then improvise by adding action and words to explore what might happen next. You can pause them by hitting an imaginary 'freeze' button and then hitting an 'action' button to restart the improvisation.

Session 7 Read on until the magician's comment, "He has probably been eaten". Ask students to walk around the room in role as guests at Fioran and Feolf's wedding. Who are they? Courtiers? Rich lords or ladies from a neighbouring kingdom? How did they travel to the wedding? What gifts did they decide on? When they've walked around the room and become used to their roles, ask them to stop and chat with a nearby guest about Feolf's non-appearance. What do they imagine has happened to the knight? You can then enter the drama as a guest who's been held up on the way and ask some of the other guests (now indignant) what on earth has happened. Later, after debriefing, ask students to write their version of the occasion.

Session 8 Read the next opening. In four groups (ladies-in-waiting, jesters, minstrels and cooks), have students develop a sound and movement sequence to represent the gradual descent of silence and gloom on the castle as Fioran remains inconsolable.

Session 9 Finish reading the story. Discuss with students the themes it raises. Are they satisfied with the resolution? Is it similar to the predictions they made?

Note: This drama sequence can be enhanced if it forms part of a unit exploring fairy-tale narrative, or knights and legends, or the Middle Ages. Many related activities in all the learning areas can be usefully integrated. In English, for example, students could develop a story map by expanding their initial sculptures or images. They might need to research some of the vocabulary in order to understand the richness of the language Jenny Wagner has used. In Studies of Society and Environment, they might research the period in which the story is set in order to assume their roles as minstrels, jesters etc. more authentically. Or they might choose to concentrate on a particular aspect of life, such as food, dress or transport. In Music, they might need to listen to recordings of the lute, harp or rebec, or medieval songs performed with an instrumental ensemble.

THE GREAT BEAR

Suitability   Years 5–7
Duration   Six sessions of 50 minutes each

Anticipated outcomes

Students will develop the ability to:
- discuss abstract concepts such as freedom, cruelty and triumph over adversity
- interpret images and subtexts
- use prediction skills
- work collaboratively
- reflect on their choices and expectations.

Focus

The notion of bullying, and the responses of people who are bullied.

Note: Given the nature of this book, the information (mostly in the illustrations) is released for the drama in planned chunks, rather than in one reading.

Before reading this text, it would be useful to look at the legends surrounding some of the constellations in both the northern and southern hemispheres.

Session 1 Examine the cover and pool the associations suggested by the title, the images of the stars and the medieval faces. Using the illustration of the medieval crowd awaiting the bear as a springboard, have students discuss who the people might be, and the mood of each. Groups of five students then choose and duplicate some of the chosen characters from the picture. Tap in to hear what each character is anticipating about the performance of the bear.

Session 2 Invite students to examine the picture showing the circus troupe approaching a walled medieval town. Ask them to imagine they are part of this troupe. What sort of a performer would they be? Acrobat? Bear trainer? Strong man? How confident is their character about performing? Then ask them to form two lines outside the town (represented by one of the classroom walls), with the most confident closest to the wall, and the least confident furthest away. As you walk down this 'conscience alley', ask each character to speak aloud their feelings about performing in this town tonight.

Session 3 Form students into small groups of performers, and ask them to prepare (as a still image) a poster that will advertise them as a family group about to enter the town. They can represent a mixture of performers, but they must include a performing bear, represented by an empty chair. In turns, they present their poster, with one member (or the group) speaking aloud a prepared 'spiel' to go with the poster.

Session 4 Prior to this session, gather three-dimensional objects that replicate the objects drawn by Armin Greder in the middle pages of the book — objects dropped by the people as they try to escape the bear (scarf, hat, stones, sticks, bag, shoe, belt, basket). Place them in the middle of the focus circle, and invite groups of two or three to select one object. The group discusses how one of the characters (from the cover) obtained this object, and why they had it while waiting for the bear. Ask one volunteer from each group to become part of a hot-seating panel which responds to questions about their expectations of the performance of the dancing bear.

Session 5 From this point, the book has no words, only double-page illustrations. Slowly but steadily, turn the pages after the moment when the bear turns on the crowd. Give the students time to absorb and interpret the images for themselves. At the conclusion, ask: "If the bear doesn't die in making this leap, what could it mean? Show me, in any drama form you like, how it could be interpreted." Students negotiate and present responses (e.g. improvisations, still images, mime) aimed at interpreting the leap into the sky, perhaps tapping into the myth of the Great Bear constellation.

Session 6 Spend some time debriefing and talking about the drama experience. Ask students to write a journal entry describing how they felt.

Programming drama in other learning areas

> A drama teacher needs to be adaptable, to look for possibilities and explore the unknown (Darvall, 1992:21).

Any issue can be explored with the aid of drama strategies. A unit on Antarctica, for example, might examine the potential threat to the environment posed by the establishment of a tourist resort. Once students' field knowledge of the Antarctic has been developed, they could take on roles as groups of scientists, environmentalists and corporate executives. The ensuing debate (in role) could help the students to understand that such issues are never black or white, and that everybody brings to them their own interests and experiences.

Drama can be used inventively for teaching space concepts in Maths. For example, you might take on the role of a sales representative from a well-known manufacturer of playground equipment to brief the students on redesigning a section of their playground using items from the catalogues you've brought with you. The catalogues would include illustrations, prices and dimensions for all items. The students might work in small groups to develop a questionnaire seeking to identify the needs of students in other classes, then work within a set budget to design, document and justify their solution.

HOW WE USED DRAMA IN CROSS-CURRICULAR STUDY

I used 'The Burnt Stick' as a starting point for my Year 5 students to explore issues related to the stolen generation, which formed part of a Studies of Society unit. Initially we looked at newspaper articles to build up students' field knowledge of the issues related to the topic. Students then brainstormed words that described 'home' to them, before depicting how they would feel if they were taken from home and knew they would never be allowed to return. We structured this as voice collage: each student read their word to convey as much emotion as they could.

As we read the story together, students used coloured oil pastels to draw their impressions of Pearl Bay Mission, and contrasted these with charcoal sketches of Dryborough Station (see page iv). Later, small groups decided on three critical moments from the story to depict, and they shared these with the class. We photographed these depictions, and students used them later to write captions of the moments they had chosen in the story.

We had a class discussion on the justifications and problems inherent in taking indigenous children from their families. Students drew up a Plus-Minus-Interesting chart (see page 114 for an example). This led to some modelling of writing an expository text. Finally, each student wrote five words describing what reconciliation now meant to them. These words were later transferred to cut-outs of their hand and displayed.

I was impressed with the way the drama strategies we used allowed them to see the perspective of John — who was taken from his mother at five — alongside the perspectives of the man from Welfare and the station owner's wife.

    Peter, Year 5 teacher

References and sources

Apple, M (1990) *Ideology and Curriculum* 2nd edn. Routledge, New York.

Connor, J, Murdoch, K et al. (2002) *Practical Literacy Programming*. Primary English Teaching Association, Sydney.

Darvall, L (1992) *Drama and the Curriculum*. Deakin University Press, Geelong.

Education Queensland (2002) *New Basics: Theory into Practice*. Education Queensland, Brisbane.

Finn, B (chair) (1991) *Young People's Participation in Post Compulsory Education & Training*. Report of the Australian Education Council Committee, Canberra.

Gleeson, L & Greder, A (1999) *The Great Bear*. Scholastic, Sydney.

Hill, A (1995) *The Burnt Stick*. Puffin, Melbourne.

Mayer, E, (chair) (1992) *Employment Related Key Competencies: A Proposal for Consultation*. Owen King, Melbourne.

Neelands, J (1990) *Structuring Drama Work*. Cambridge University Press, Cambridge.

NSW Department of Education and Training (2003) *Quality Teaching: A Discussion Paper*. NSW DET, Sydney.

Spady, W (1992) *Outcomes-Based Education*. Australian Curriculum Studies, Melbourne.

Waddell, M & Oxenbury, H (1991) *Farmer Duck*. Walker, London.

Wagner, J & Roennfeldt, R (1995) *The Werewolf Knight*. Mark Macleod, Random House, Sydney.

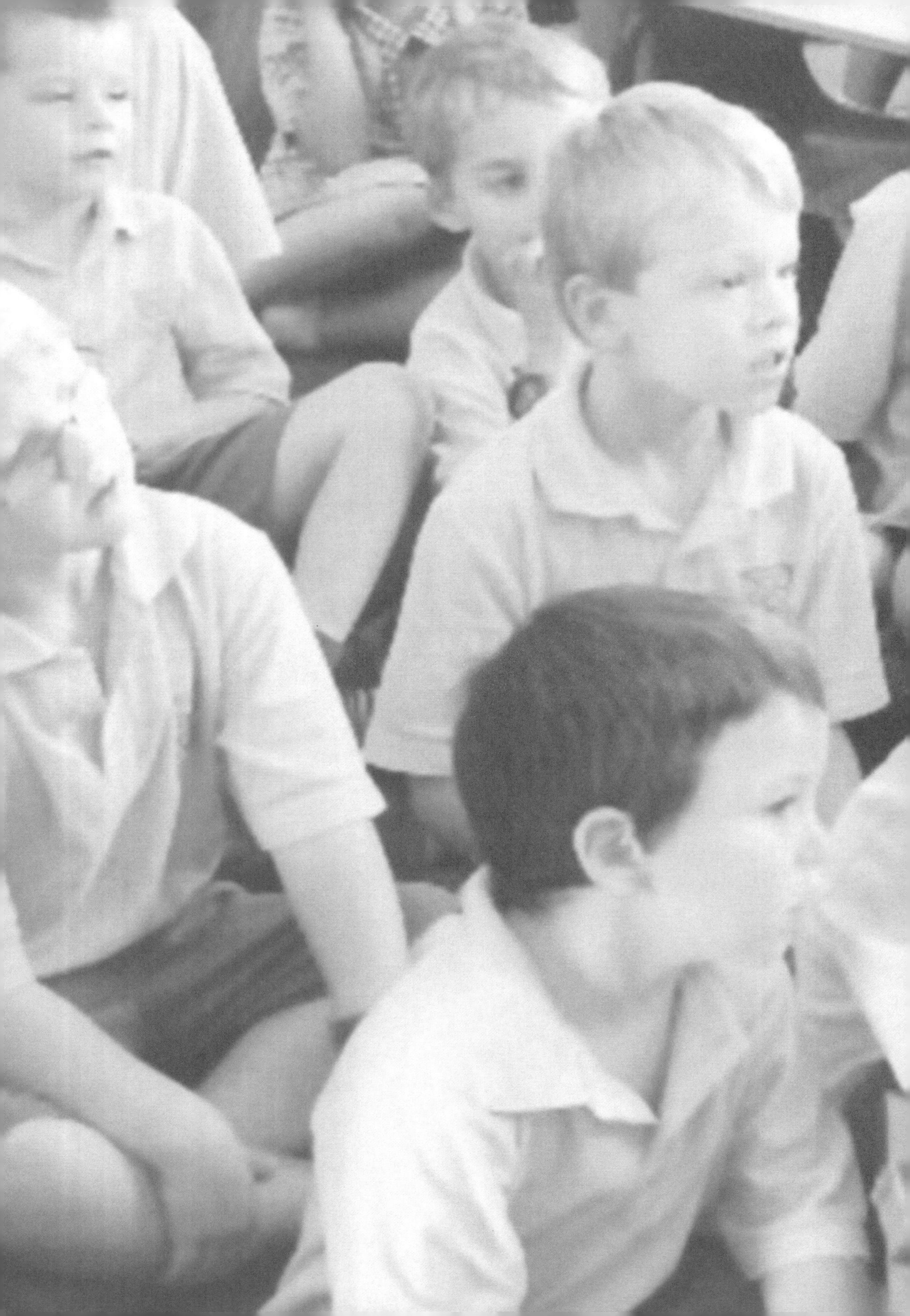

CHAPTER SIX

Puppetry

Puppetry is almost as old as civilisation itself. A puppet is any object brought to life by a person. It's this life — transferred from the handler to the puppet and communicated to an audience — that creates the magic of puppetry. Young children often animate dolls, toys and other objects spontaneously; they become puppeteers, without prompting, from an early age. The puppet can be as simple as a box or a stick, as long as it takes on a character distinct from that of its animator. Part of the never-ending appeal of puppetry lies in the fact that the puppet is the focus of attention, and so the puppeteer feels safe.

Puppetry is in some ways a microcosm of the drama process; it is both an art form and a teaching/learning tool across the curriculum. Students can practise oral and written story-telling, discuss the scripting and production of a play, and extend their imagination as audience members. By making a wide range of puppets from 'junk' (sticks, pieces of cloth, egg cartons etc.), they can develop their awareness of how an inanimate object can symbolise a particular character or concept. If they go beyond junk puppetry, they can investigate more sophisticated methods of design and construction. At other times, they might research a particular era or historical event in detail, or they might select appropriate music and sounds — especially if they're taking a play to performance. All the while, students develop their abilities to co-operate and concentrate, and they gain experience in manipulating the puppet they've created.

Working with puppets encourages people to express their feelings, and it can provide a release valve for some students. It's this quality of puppetry that has caused it to be used on occasion as a counselling aid, encouraging children to share things that they may be unable to express directly.

The puppet as metaphor

A metaphor is a comparison of two things whereby one is said to *be* the other: for example, "He is a lion among men". Puppets can operate metaphorically: they can be said to *be* feelings or character traits (e.g. happiness, love, fear), objects (e.g. trees, rocks), or symbols (e.g. coats of arms, flags), as well as humans or animals. Puppets are constructed from materials chosen because of their potential to represent some aspect of a character or thing, or its essence; thus a stern soldier might be suggested by a rigid torso made of sticks; a flighty character might have a body of floating, chiffon-like material. The materials that make up the puppet come to stand for the chosen character. As such, a puppet is

> both an essence and an emphasis ... it is more than its live counterpart — simpler, sadder, more wicked, more supple. At the same time, it may be less complex than the character it represents. A mere suggestion has caused the puppet to be filled with life and exert a universal appeal (Educational Drama Association, 1981:1).

Thus it's important for students to invest each of their puppets with a name, and with particular ways of speaking and moving that are the essence of the chosen character. Finding the correct tone and pitch for a puppet's speech, and determining how it relates to other puppets, is part of filling out the comparison.

Types of puppets

Puppetry gives people scope to choose the medium best suited to the concept or theme to be dramatised. Many types of puppets lend themselves to classroom use, and they are briefly described below.

Finger puppets. Often the most appropriate for younger students, finger puppets can be knitted, or made from toy felt that is sewn or glued together. Alternatively, they can be drawn or duplicated on stiff coloured paper with a 'ground level' strip to form a ring around the finger. Distractions during story-telling can be minimised if the students manipulate their finger characters while you, or another student, reads or tells the story.

Paper-plate puppets. To simplify the logistics of minor dramatic productions, characters can be made out of paper plates attached to a ruler or a piece of firm cardboard to make manipulation easier. The script or outline for the performance can be stuck on the back.

Shadow puppets. Shadows formed by hands or cut-out figures can easily be projected onto a wall or screen. The easiest way to begin is with 'fuzzy felt' or paper figures, perhaps with cellophane-filled cut-outs to add colour on the overhead projector. To avoid hand shadows, students can manipulate the figures with knitting needles or sticks fixed to the back. Simple scenery drawn on acetate sheets — perhaps coloured — can also be placed on the overhead projector.

Hand or glove puppets. These are the most versatile and popular puppets of all. They are probably the best to use for scripted plays, when stages, scenery etc. can be used as well. While heads can be made from a variety of materials (e.g. papier mache, or fabric), the polystyrene-ball method is recommended for uniformity of product and speed of construction. Students can each make a puppet at the beginning of the year to provide a class or school set. This will encourage the frequent use of puppets in improvisation, as well as in more formal activities across all learning areas. An effective puppet theatre can be constructed out of a cardboard box used to package a washing machine, fridge or computer.

Ventriloquial puppets. Ventriloquial puppets make frequent appearances on children's television programs, and they're often used as learning tools with students in early-years classrooms. They are appealing to children and adults alike.

Marionettes and rod puppets. These are generally too complicated for primary students to make easily, and in any case they don't lend themselves to classroom use.

Masks. Masks are listed here because they serve as inanimate representations of people or ideas drawn from life. Masks make actors more puppet-like, denying or restricting their use of one of their most expressive features — their face. Full-face masks can of course be decorated more elaborately than half-face or eye masks. Masks can also be reduced even further — to labels stuck on foreheads, paper bird beaks taped to noses or red clown noses attached with elastic — and they can be labelled as objects, concepts, numerals or names.

It's beyond the scope of this chapter to examine puppet construction in any detail. However, craft books abound with instructions on how to make a range of puppets, from junk puppets to more formal and longer-lasting ones.

Beginning with puppets in the classroom

Puppets can be used to improvise, mime, dance, perform a scripted play, or even perform a circus. The suggestions that follow assume that students have already made a puppet, either from junk materials or more carefully, over a period of time, as part of an arts- or technology-based unit.

Movement and space. Divide the students into pairs and ask them to imagine that A's hand or foot is shy, and B's hand or foot is trying to make friends. What movements will they make in relation to each other? Then ask them to imagine that A's hand or foot is an alien, to which B's is making a friendly approach. How will they interact? Ask them to repeat the sequence using puppets.

Voice. Ask the students to introduce their puppet to the group, including a name and a few facts, and using variations of pitch, accent, pace and tone appropriate to the character. For instance, a lion may speak at a low pitch, and if she's an aggressive lion, that will affect the tone of her voice. How will she speak if she's anxious, or in a hurry?

Imagination. Ask the students to have one-sided conversations with their puppets: they do the talking and the puppets simply move, as if in response.

Improvisation. Have students form groups of four with their puppets. Ask them to use the following questions as a framework to decide:

- *Who* are the puppets?
- *Where* are they?
- *When* is the action happening?
- *Why* are the puppets together?

They could then prepare a story map, either as a group or individually, for their agreed scenario.

Rehearsal. To develop the scenario further, ask the groups to prepare and present an improvisation to the rest of the class. You might want to supply some guidelines (e.g. a focus on the concept of friendship, or the theme of the sea).

Staging a puppet play

Students need lots of opportunities for spontaneous improvisation with puppets before they're ready to stage a more formal performance. However, when they are ready, there are a number of principles to bear in mind.

Develop the play from students' improvisations. If you use a prepared script, your students won't 'own' the dialogue or action. When they're creating their own script, suggest that they keep the plot simple and include no more than three or four main characters.

Concentrate on action. A lot of dialogue will distract performers from manipulating their puppets. Puppet movements need to be large and to make use of the whole puppet stage. Encouraging students to practise larger-than-life movements in front of a mirror can be helpful.

Tape the script prior to performance. It's hard for students to project their voices and simultaneously concentrate on puppet action. Taping the script in advance gets around this problem and allows them to think more critically about their characters' voices. Sound effects and music between scenes can also be included more easily.

Minimise stage directions and scene changes. Impromptu stages can be simply constructed. A table with a cloth or blanket draped over it, a large cardboard box or a windowsill can all suffice. Backdrops can have cardboard cut-outs pinned to them. Simple, natural stage directions and minimal scene changes will enable students to concentrate on their puppet characters.

Use props for symbolism rather than realism. Although props needn't be realistic, they do need to be in scale with the puppets. Doll's-house furniture can sometimes be adapted.

Use overhead lighting. Torches or angle lamps can be effective. Even the light from a slide projector may do the job. You can also try an overhead projector.

WHAT WE DO

I often set the making of a junk puppet as a homework project to be done over a couple of weeks by students in my composite class of school beginners. I stress in my letter to parents that while the children may need assistance, it should be their puppet — not one made by Mum or Dad. At the same time, I suggest it needs to be durable enough for frequent class use.

I'm constantly amazed at how helpful puppetry can be for students. They just feel initially more comfortable if they can transfer the dramatic process to their puppet. When my students introduce their puppets to the larger group for the first time, some speak more confidently than in any other speaking context.

Here's an excerpt from a script developed by two of my students. It emerged out of the 'Beginning with puppets' activity sequence described above.

>Gai, early-years teacher

Storyteller: One day a Burmese cat with orange fur and a mouse with a long tail went for a walk across the road. They weren't together because they weren't friends.

Cat: Yum ... That mouse looks delicious!

Storyteller: The cat chased the mouse into a dead end.

Mouse: Oh no ... I'm stuck!

Storyteller: The cat gobbled up the mouse.

Cat: Yum. (*Yawns*) I feel sleepy now. I think I'll have a nap now.

Storyteller: The mouse decided to chew his way out of the greedy cat because he had swallowed him whole.

Mouse: Now I'll tie this cat up with string so he can't do it again.

References and sources

Educational Drama Association (1981) *Puppetry*. Educational Drama Association, NSW.

French, R & French, J (1991) *Puppet Drama*. ANZEA, Sydney.

Sinclair, A (1996) *The Puppetry Handbook*. Richard Lee, Castlemaine.

CHAPTER SEVEN

Playbuilding

Playbuilding is a process which combines a range of techniques in such a way that students can explore in depth important issues across the curriculum. In playbuilding, students create the drama as they watch themselves and others participating in it. The ability to be simultaneously an actor and a detached observer is called *metaxis*. Through it, students develop affective understandings of important issues. It is the double-knowing of metaxis that makes learning possible in improvised drama, because "what is submitted to passively is also actively construed and reflected upon" (Bolton, 1984:162).

Playbuilding can begin with a general issue (e.g. caring for pets) or a specific question (e.g. "Why was Alison Ashley such a goody-goody?"). Alternatively it can begin with resources chosen because they intrigue the students — arousing their interest and curiosity, and motivating them to explore a related theme. Closely examining a photograph of a strong, interesting face is a good way to launch a character-based role play; introducing a three-dimensional object with texture and colour can evoke a strong, affective response. Facts can be seen in a new light as they are processed through dramatic experience.

The playbuilding process

All of the techniques described in earlier chapters (e.g. teacher in role, mantle of the expert, still image, improvisation) can be used in playbuilding. Those selected are adapted to the chosen theme, and sections of the drama are interlinked in such a way that the whole becomes more than the sum of its parts. However, there's no step-by-step model to follow, and your decisions about how the various techniques are put together are crucial to success.

Let's assume, for example, that your students want to playbuild on the broad topic of pets. In the process, you might assist them to hot-seat pet owners, sculpt scenes where some of these owners love (or hate) their animals, and improvise a scene at an RSPCA shelter. As the playbuilding proceeds, you will be rapidly reflecting in action: you might subtly focus students' attention on a small detail mentioned during the hot-seating, redirect focus after the sculptings, or link the episodes by a narration that moves the story into the future. By these means you seek to deepen their understandings, or to add layers of complexity that move the scenario away from stereotyped patterns. Sometimes you may want to involve your class directly in this sort of manoeuvre, laying the process bare with questions like: "Do we want to see what happens to this cruel child ten years from now?". That sort of negotiation will depend on the maturity and experience of your students.

Playbuilding can be a much longer process than students are used to. It often continues over several sessions, and may involve research. In some sessions, students may need to recall what's already happened, and an option here is to begin each lesson by revisiting 'the story so far', using drama techniques like round-the-circle stories or a series of still images.

The material that emerges from playbuilding needn't be presented to an outside audience; the 'play' may well remain incipient, with students electing to leave the process at the experiential level. The process is similar to the rehearsal phase of a professional play, where actors experiment with the material to develop their own understanding. If, however, the ultimate intention is to perform for others, the focus of the work shifts to communicating these understandings to an audience. Hot-seating, for example, is a powerful technique for playbuilding: it strongly engages the participants in the process and may enable them to penetrate a particular character's motives. However, that doesn't mean it's necessarily the best technique for performance. Involving an outside audience may be done more effectively by converting the content of the hot-seating into scripted dialogue.

Playbuilding, then, can either be a classroom process, where the participants create a 'play' for themselves, or part of a continuum leading to the blocking, scripting and performance of a play for an audience.

Introducing and teaching playbuilding

Playbuilding uses all the elements of drama discussed in Chapter 1: role, focus, tension and symbol. Any playbuilding process involves several essential steps, and these are described below.

Choosing the topic

Almost any unit or topic in any learning area can be explored through playbuilding. Dorothy Heathcote typically began the process by asking: "What do you want to do a play about?". This may be the right kind of beginning for an experienced group of students. For instance, one Year 4 boy, faced with this question, came up with "Wardrobes". His teacher was initially taken aback, but a little discussion soon revealed why wardrobes were so important to him. His parents had recently separated, and he was angry at spending so much time between their two houses, packing and unpacking into different wardrobes. Subsequently, a play was developed about relationships, divorce and its effect on children. The initial suggestion had provided a stimulus to open up some issues that were genuinely important — and not just for that one student.

Generating ideas

Unless you can help your students to go beyond what they already know, the potential of playbuilding will be wasted. The process often involves researching the topic — finding such things as pictures, stories or newspaper articles that open it up. You might collect some of these with the idea of introducing them at suitable moments; others will be gathered by the students as part of their exploration.

Finding a symbol

The best resources are those capable of becoming symbols. Exploring the symbolic object helps to establish meaning in the drama. Symbols can link students' particular ideas and actions with the experiences of other humans in other places and times. So, for example, a student in role as a new settler who chooses and then carries a family photograph as a keepsake can link his/her emotions with immigrants across the ages who suffer homesickness as they seek a new life in a strange land.

Repeatedly using a symbolic object helps the students to apprehend that several meanings can operate simultaneously. A group of students creating an adventure on an uninhabited island may also be exploring, at a symbolic level, what is involved in establishing and maintaining a good community (see the 'Holiday Island' workshop later in this chapter). A specific issue arising in the drama (e.g. an argument about the use of a skateboard) can become a metaphor with a broader application (e.g. the importance of observing documented rules). By planning for this double layer of meaning, you will ensure that students engage in worthwhile learning.

A symbolic object allows students to see the physical equivalent of a less tangible concept, and can reinforce the theme. For example, in the drama 'The Baby on the Train' (Nicholson, 2001), different groups of students were asked to use the same resource — a bundle of baby blankets — when enacting still images and improvisations about a family under pressure. The repeated use of the symbolic object reinforced the centrality of the baby to the different narratives being constructed; it also enabled the groups to compile a single story that had the baby's welfare as its centre.

While the topic must be concerned with specific people and places (the fiction), it also needs to extend beyond these specifics to a more broadly applicable meaning (the metaphor). One of your aims in structuring the process is to help students to link their own lives by metaphor to the themes they're exploring. The playbuilding might appear to be about Antarctic exploration, for example, but more importantly, students could be exploring such notions as ambition, teamwork and environmental stewardship. So, although the context may be historical on the surface, the metaphorical extension enables them to apply understandings with direct relevance to their own lives.

Establishing identities

Instead of exploring the thematic content first, students can begin the playbuilding process by establishing a role or identity. There are at least three ways to do this.

Mime allows students to represent a fictional identity. It can be applied in co-operative contexts such as:

- working in a mine
- making toys in a factory
- working as a group of clowns in a circus troupe.

The mime could lead students into a deeper exploration of who their characters are and what circumstances they might encounter.

Still images can help to establish identities. Here's a useful one.

> In groups of four, decide which family member you would like to be, and then work out how each of you would stand for a family portrait.

Students can then think about how their family member would walk, talk and behave, and brief improvisations can build up the characters before they are asked to write a journal entry in role.

Movement offers another way of finding an identity. For example, you could ask students to move around the room in a particular way (e.g. through mud, using different levels, taking huge/tiny steps). You could then ask them to imagine who they are that they might be moving in this way, and to stop and talk (in role) to the person beside them. The accumulated roles might become a particular crowd (e.g. witnesses to an accident) that forms a springboard to playbuilding.

Responding to objects

Objects can sometimes suggest dramatic contexts for playbuilding. For example:

- an 'old' map (made by dyeing paper in tea and burning the edges) may be the beginning of a play about what motivates and sustains explorers
- an old coin could be the focus of suggestions about why people go off in search of hidden treasure.

A particularly striking painting, text illustration or photograph can provide a similar stimulus.

Responding to music or lyrics

A particular piece of music or the words of a popular song may evoke a setting, event or character which becomes the context for playbuilding (e.g. the national anthem may suggest an event at the Olympics).

Building on a 'pre-text'

Since the mid nineties, the term 'pre-text' has been applied to a text selected to "activate the weaving of the text of the drama" (O'Neill, cited in Taylor, 2000: 25). A good pre-text will not only suggest possible characters, contexts and situations, it will lure students into a willing exploration of an imagined world. The motivational power of a pre-text is an important characteristic. Pre-texts can be written texts, oral stories, maps, diagrams, pictures, television news clips, pieces of music, sections from a newspaper, three-dimensional objects, pieces of material or articles of clothing.

Exploring 'spaces' in a text

Oblique or implicit references in a text can be worth investigating. Students might speculate about the fate of the Wild Things after Max sails home (in *Where the Wild Things Are*), or explore Princess Fioran's reaction when Feolf tells her that he is a werewolf (in *The Werewolf Knight*). Each collage in *Window* could be brought to life using the view from the window as a starting point.

A Year 2 class that studied *Oi! Get Off Our Train* listed other endangered animals that were not mentioned in the text — animals that could equally well have demanded a seat on the little boy's train. The students researched an animal they had chosen. Over several sessions, they were all hot-seated in role as their chosen animal before creating their own appeal to be allowed to stay on the train. Finn, for example, wrote:

> **Please let me come with you on your train. All the gum trees where I live are dying and soon there will be none of us left.**

Later, a readers' theatre script included each child's text, masks were made and a series of movements were choreographed for eventual performance to the whole school.

Scaffolding ideas

Whichever strategy you use to spark ideas, scaffolding them is vital to the development of the play. When you scaffold a drama, you build a framework that enables your students to move beyond the concepts they're expected to be familiar with. Using prompts, cues or carefully constructed questions, you can assist in breaking up problems in such a way that your students can deal effectively with each segment.

Scaffolding works if you know and understand your students and have a clear focus or direction for the learning experience. However, sometimes it is the students who contribute most to the learning. In a series of team-teaching sessions, Jennifer and Louise Quirk supported playbuilding activities in which the focus was survival/disaster. The students ranged in age from 5 to 14. The play was based on a train smash. In one early episode, the students decided that the cause of the crash could have been the incompetence of the signal operators, and this led to the question of how the operators had been trained. The students established a railway school: some were selected to tutor the others on how to become competent signal operators. When the tutors met separately to draw up plans for teaching signalling, Jennifer expected them to devise a flag system based her own childhood experience of trains, but they set up the training on a computer-controlled system. The challenge had spurred them to apply their knowledge of today's world to an old situation.

Edging into drama

When you're working on drama where emotions will be strongly engaged, it's important to use the fictional context as a protective device. For example, in dealing with a topic like 'How important is friendship in your life?' as part of the Personal Development curriculum, you might ask your class to draw sociograms of the friends they have and then think about other ways in which people can be friends. Because drama is very public, collaborative work, you might explore the question by asking the class to think about two imaginary friends involved in an argument. Establishing a fictional context protects the students; it frees them to bring what they know about the world to this new situation without putting themselves too much on the line. They're still going to explore the notion of friendship, but the risk is reduced because they're working with fictional characters. Those who find it difficult to make friends might create or select a fictional character who shares their difficulty. Those who've developed some successful techniques for making friends will bring these qualities to the drama, too.

Here are some other ways of edging into drama.

Hot-seating can ease students into the fictional world. Any character in a text or drama can be picked out for interview, and students can work in buzz groups to prepare questions to put to the character chosen.

Rituals can be introduced to build belief in the fictional context. For instance:

> You will tell nobody of our decision to kill the inhabitants of Jupiter. Swear this solemn oath not to betray our secret!

This ritual exemplifies the principle of imposing constraint — a tension-building technique discussed in Chapter 1.

Teacher in role enables you to enter the drama with a different viewpoint from that expressed by the students. This will help you to deepen the drama or assess the students' commitment to what's being created. Remember to think about your status when you choose your role. For example:

> Excuse me, I'm very late. My carriage lost a wheel in a ditch ... but tell me, why is the Queen crying?

> OR

> They told me that the palace cleaners might know what's happened to all the spinning wheels. I need mine to make a living.

Both of these scenarios allow you to step out of your accustomed role as expert knower and bestow it on your students, who are then challenged to share their knowledge of a particular story or context.

Playbuilding in action

The following playbuilding sequence is based on a series of workshop sessions undertaken with a group of students in the later years of primary school.

Holiday Island

Session 1

Begin with a large island shape drawn on the board. Explain that the class is going to create its own holiday island, one entirely operated for rest and relaxation. Tell the students that you will adopt the role of the island's tourist officer, and that they will become people who are visiting the resort. (The roles they adopt at this point are 'shadow roles' — they are not yet necessarily people other than themselves, but they accept the fiction of being in another place.)

Begin with "Good morning. I know that yesterday you all had a chance to explore the island, so I wonder if today you might like to share with the group some of the things you saw and did, and perhaps you can place it on this big map for other people to see." Here you can pause and wait for a response (usually it takes at least seven seconds!). You may need to add: "Did anyone visit the beach? Where was it on the island?"

As students respond with their imaginary experiences, fill the map in. (It will probably be composed of things that the students would wish for, and this is highly motivating for the drama.) You can add tension to some of the suggestions, for example: "I hope you saw the warning on the beach that there are sharks further out, so I caution you not to swim there alone, or to go beyond the nets." At the end of this session, your students have created a 'holiday island'.

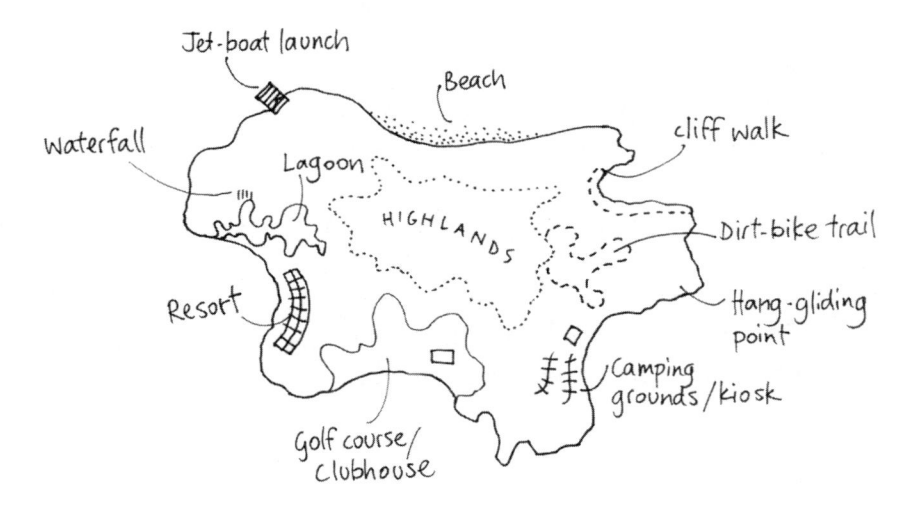

Session 2

Have small groups of students prepare improvisations of advertisements that Holiday Island will use to attract customers. These will be used to draw attention to its different attractions; for example, someone could be swimming in the lagoon, which has a waterfall. Of course, these ads will not show the less attractive side of any attraction! The ads might include an appropriate song. Ask each group to rehearse and present an improvisation lasting no more than one minute. (To extend the drama, give the groups time to produce video advertisements. They could view and critique their ads as examples of screen drama. They could also establish a website for Holiday Island using these recorded vignettes and stills.)

Session 3

Invite each student to choose a role by selecting a face cut from a magazine. Ensure that there are no famous faces, and that there are more pictures than students, so that they have a choice of role. Ask each student, based on their chosen photo, to adopt the stance of a person on the island. Next, have them 'role-walk' around the room, perhaps to music, each deciding why s/he is on the island, and how s/he feels about it. They stop on a sound signal from you and, in role, introduce themselves to other characters nearby, sharing their reasons for being on the island, and their expectations. In pairs, they flesh out the identity of their character and write the name on a role card. They then come back into a focus circle, and are introduced in role to the group of other holiday makers.

Session 4

Arrange for a panel of characters to be put in the 'hot seat' — questioned in role about problems they've encountered on the island. Support the questioners to 'lead' these characters with a proposition that they must accept or reject. For example, a leading question could be: "Is it true that you caught a thief in one of the rooms of the hotel?". (Remember that the purpose of questions in hot-seating is not to trip up the students in role, but to collaborate with them by making suggestions that help them to create an interesting situation or character. You may have to model the questioning technique.)

Session 5

Suggest that students role-play a meeting that's been called to discuss the island's problems. Tell them that you are switching to a new role: assistant manager of the island. Put on a colourful scarf to signify the change, then move quickly in role into this scene.

> I'm Ms O'Reilly, assistant manager. They tell me you want to talk to the manager, but she's missed her flight. She's asked me to apologise and wants us to start the meeting without her. Now, I believe some of you are upset?

Elicit some of the complaints. However, gradually reveal, through subtext, that you are refusing to accept responsibility. The status that you have adopted (second in charge) means you can be sympathetic, but you must refer them to 'the boss' or 'the board' for a decision. This session is highly unpredictable in terms of student responses, emerging tensions and direction. Finally, out of role, the students return to the focus circle in order to reflect on the drama. Invite them to de-role by sharing how they felt inside their roles, and by reflecting on interactions between other members of the group. Then invite them to write in role for different sections of the local newspaper — for example, front-page news, social columns or business pages. These reflections form part of your evaluation of the success of the drama, together with observations, the photos or video, and other forms of documentation.

Reflecting on playbuilding

It's essential to provide opportunities for reflecting on both the process and content of playbuilding. Provide time to talk about the important issues that were focused on, as well as opportunities to respond through journal-writing, drawing or painting after each drama session. Personal reflections and more universal responses are both significant (see Chapter 11). In addition, students might consider how they found the actual process and how they felt they responded to it.

WHAT WE DID

I used playbuilding with my Year 6 class to discuss the fears they were having about going to secondary school. Initially they drew a map of an imaginary secondary school before developing small group improvisations around what might happen on the first day. A number of these reflected their concerns: getting lost trying to find a room; being bullied by a group of older students. It helped me understand how they were feeling about moving from the security of primary school. We then developed positive scenarios to put alongside the others.

During debriefing, we discussed what they might do if things started to go wrong. In a later session, they went back to the darker scenarios and built in an active response to getting lost, being bullied, and so on.

Jenny, upper-primary teacher

References and sources

Baker, J (1991) *Window*. Julia MacRae, London.

Bolton, G (1984) *Drama as Education*. Longman, London.

Burningham, J (1989) *Oi! Get Off Our Train*. Random House, London.

Simons, J (2000) 'Walking in Another Person's Shoes: Storytellling and Roleplay'. In Nicholson, H (ed.), *Teaching Drama 11–16*. Continuum, London.

Sendak, M (1962) *Where the Wild Things Are*. Harper & Row, New York.

Taylor, P (2000) *The Drama Classroom: Action Reflection through Transformation*. Falmer Press, London.

Wagner, J (1995) *The Werewolf Knight*. Mark Macleod, Random House, Sydney.

CHAPTER EIGHT

Storying

> The fact of storytelling hints at a fundamental human unease,
> hints at human imperfection.
> Where there is perfection, there is no story to tell.
>
> Ben Okri, *Birds of Heaven*

Storying> is part of being human. We live our lives, celebrate them and make sense of who we are through story. Children are initiated into their culture through story. Thirty years ago, Barbara Hardy (1975:4-5) argued that narrative was "a primary act of mind, transferred to art from life". From an early age, children are capable of storying — using the stories they hear and tell to sort out their own knowledge and ideas, establish who they are in relation to others, even assess other people's impressions of them. It is, then, a sad indictment of our Western education systems that so little formal emphasis is placed on storying and story-telling. Kieran Egan (2003) has recently suggested that curriculum has become too constrained by building on children's prior knowledge while ignoring their imaginative lives and capacities.

> > The term is used here to mean the use of narrative to develop, construct and relate ideas (Lowe, 2002) — something that includes, but goes beyond, story-telling.

Oral story-telling

Oral story-telling is often an important precursor to the development of other literacy capabilities. Carol Fox, who has documented (1983, 1993) many of the oral narratives of young children, demonstrated that they learn to 'talk like a book'. This chapter initially discusses the importance of including story-telling as an integral part of the classroom before focusing on drama strategies that will help students nurture and communicate their own stories.

Is story-telling a regular feature of your classroom? Do you tell stories? Do your students? The recent focus on elements of 'productive pedagogy' or 'quality teaching' highlights the need for narrative to be an important feature of all classrooms because it helps students to connect what's happening in the classroom with the real world. Both the reading and the telling of stories are important and, as Colwell (1991) has pointed out, there's an enormous difference between them. A person *telling* a story is able to speak directly and spontaneously, and watch for listeners' responses. A person *reading* a story, on the other hand, is always constrained by the printed text and the author's sequence and imagination.

Different orientations to sharing stories

Children often come to school with a strong sense of story, although what kind of sense they bring will depend on their background. As a teacher, you have to be careful to value different sorts of stories. There's a lot of research, particularly from the United States, which suggests that teachers tend to be middle-class in orientation, favouring stories that embody middle-class values. Thus they may implicitly put down or devalue stories from students who don't share others' economic privilege. There's also evidence to suggest that story-telling forms for different cultures are quite different. For example, Indigenous Australians often tell stories that don't conform to the story structure described by genrists.

Many children begin school without any developed knowledge of the traditional stories, fairy tales, myths and legends that we often assume to have been part of their childhood socialisation. Their sense of carrying 'inferior' knowledge is all the greater if the school doesn't give them access to stories from outside the Western tradition.

Teachers often express a lack of confidence about story-telling (as opposed to story reading) As a result, it's not a common feature of classrooms. A study of news or sharing time in early-years classrooms in NSW (Cusworth, 1995) suggested that most teachers did not see it as an opportunity for students to share stories. Rather, it was a time to focus on technical oracy competencies. A small group of parents involved in the study also suggested that by their third year at school, many children had decided that their own personal anecdotes and experiences were not important in the classroom.

The structure of stories

Traditionally — going back to Aristotle's map of tragedy — we've been told that stories have a particular kind of shape, with a beginning, a middle and an end. In addition, many stories organise their events around a central theme or figure. Other common features include:

- causality — to establish a plot
- temporality — to locate the story in time
- context — to situate the story.

Genre theorists (e.g. Martin & Rothery, 1982) have suggested that narratives are texts which contain an orientation, a dilemma or complication, and a resolution. Yet oral narratives don't necessarily fit into such a linear framework (nor, come to that, do written ones). Teaching and learning must allow room for open-ended sorts of narrative that don't have a conventional resolution. After all, lots of stories do finish open-endedly, or with an unanswered question.

Story-telling starters

You can help students to build up their concept of story in many ways. A number of examples are described below.

Name games

Name games can be an effective way of helping students to play with 'facts' about their life. Gather the class in a circle and begin by saying: "My name is [a name] and I like [a preference]". You can build on this as much as you like. For example, you might ask students to start the thing that they like with the first letter of their name (e.g. "My name's Robyn and I like roses"), or to mime what they like so that everybody can try to guess what it is. The second time around, students might be asked to add some kind of description (e.g. "My name's Robyn and I like rich red roses"). Then, in pairs or small groups, they can share stories about these things and how they came to like them.

Right at the beginning of the year, when you're getting to know a particular group of students, story-telling can be particularly valuable. For instance, there are some simple games that will help you learn the names of the students in your class. See Chapter 2 for these and other name games that can be extended into story-telling opportunities.

Experiences

Instead of organising the traditional newstime, be more specific. Ask students in pairs or small groups to tell a story about, for example, their most embarrassing moment, something that went wrong, or something that happened yesterday. You might need to model the art of story-telling first, pointing out that people will commonly relate the same incidents differently. Students might have a story about a favourite relative visiting, or a time when they were lost or frightened. Ask the listener to guess whether the story is true or fictitious, or a true story that's been embellished. Depending on the experience of the group, you might suggest that tellers draw a story map first to make sure they include all the events of their story in sequence. Alternatively, a story map or storyboard might conclude the session.

Stimuli

Some teachers like to play a piece of music as a starting point for a story-telling session. Another way of beginning is to share a story about an item you're wearing and then invite continuations: "I want you to choose something that you're wearing and tell the person next to you a story about it. It doesn't have to be true. Then swap over so the other person can tell a story." Students have to decide whether the stories are true, fictitious or embellished.

Starting with a tape of a series of unrelated sounds can be extremely effective, too. Ask students to close their eyes and listen to three sounds (for example a ringing bell, a book falling on a desk, an alarm clock ticking). Ask them to interpret and suggest sources for the sounds (they don't have to be accurate). Individually or in pairs, they can then string them together to create a story.

Versions

Choose three storytellers and seat them at the front of the class. The first tells a story, the second retells the story but adds a different ending, while the third tells a different story using the same elements. Familiar fairy tales or legends can be used as a starting point for the first story. The class is then divided into three groups to mime or improvise the three stories, with the appropriate storyteller acting as narrator. If you need to divide your class into more than three groups, give one group a different task, requiring them to vary the story again or use a flashback technique. It's often effective to ask one person in a group to act as narrator while the others mime what's happening.

Role walks

Ask students to walk around the room in different ways — quickly, slowly, with tiny steps, with huge steps etc. — and to imagine who they might be (just using movement may help them to think themselves into a particular character).
Tap into these characters by freezing the movement, touching people on the shoulder and asking them to say *who* they are, *where* they're going, *how* they're dressed and *why* they're walking in this way. Put two characters together and ask them to improvise or mime a scene.

Retellings

Ask students to choose a story they'd like to retell and get them to read it as many times as they need in order to learn it. A story map can serve as a useful prompt. Story tellings can be taped to enable students to listen to themselves critically. Tellers might also like to practise in front of a mirror. See the suggested sequence over, adapted from one originally developed by Carole Miller, University of Victoria, Canada. This sequence may take several sessions.

Divide class into groups of three or four.

Assign each group a story or have groups choose one. Groups read their story silently and then discuss their initial impressions. What do individuals think the story is about?

Ask pairs to read the story aloud and discuss different impressions gained from this form of reading.

Ask students: Which moments would you choose to illustrate? Group members describe their imagined illustrations in detail.

Try a group telling, with group members taking turns to relate different sections of the story.

Refer back to the text: What was left out? Added? How are you growing the story as you bring it alive?

Have groups tell the story again, perhaps recording it.

Recombine the students in new groups. Each teller will have a story to share.

Reflect on the strengths of telling a story.

If you take the time to develop story-telling in your classroom, you'll soon find that students can translate their oral skills and begin to write stories that incorporate features like detail, motivation and characterisation. Instead of "I want you to write a story about what you did in the holidays", how much better if you can say: "I want you to walk around this room on your way to something or someone you visited in the holidays. I want you to walk the way you walked then, I want you to visualise what you were wearing that day, and I want you to think about how you were feeling on the way." Give students time to make notes about all of these things before they write their stories.

Soon after embarking on a story-telling journey in his classroom, Tony Aylwin remarked (1990:21):

> The greatest boost was the discovery that my audience didn't realise when I had missed something out. Once you know this you can concentrate on presentation,

and in this it seems to me that hanging on to the shape of the story is all-important. It is this attention to shape, I suggest, that will be a major influence on children's understanding of story in all its forms, both oral and written.

Once students are confident with the shape of their story, you can focus on the skills that help communicate a story well.

Story-telling skills

- To keep a listener interested, the storyteller needs to use an expressive *voice* which effectively conveys the mood of the story. Ask students to say the same sentence several times using the voice differently, making it sound excited, angry, tired etc.
- Students need to vary their *pace* as they tell a story, and they need to learn how to pause effectively — for example, to increase tension. Ask them to read sentences and practise pausing in different places.
- The *pitch* of the storyteller's voice helps to convey the kind of emotion being expressed. For instance, how does the pitch of an angry parent differ from that of an excited child? Students need opportunities to learn how to vary their pitch to suit particular characters. Again, have them read over the same sentence while varying their pitch.
- The expressive use of *face*, *gesture* and *movement* can enhance a story, and making eye contact with as many listeners as possible is vital.
- Attention to how a story *starts* and *ends* is also important. Encourage students to visualise the scene they're introducing — perhaps by drawing a map, painting a picture or doing some simple research before the drama begins.
- *Observation* of other storytellers provides opportunities to hear good stories. Invite a storyteller to share with your class (s/he might also contribute 'storytelling starters' that encourage students to share their own stories). You may also find that introducing *rituals* like a story chair, a teller's candle or a special scarf or hat will help to set a receptive mood in the classroom.

A story-telling workshop for older students

1. Scatter a range of objects in the middle of the floor (e.g. a candlestick, a shell and a scarf).
2. Seat the whole class in a circle around the objects and ask them to choose one.
3. Ask the students who've selected the same object to form groups and explain how they relate to the object.
4. Ask the groups to combine their ideas to construct a narrative to account for why one (fictional) person came into contact with the object.
5. Reform the students into new groups containing one member from each of the original groups (i.e. jigsaw groups) and have them share the stories created in Step 4. Create a new combined story in each jigsaw group.
6. Ask each group to mime the combined story for the whole class, narrated by one selected member (who is chosen to be the storyteller).

This workshop is an excellent introduction for a discussion of symbols in stories. What can a candle symbolise? A gold coin? A feather? It's crucial to remember that different cultural groups will value different symbols in a range of ways and this, too, is an excellent beginning for a discussion of different traditions.

A story-telling workshop for students in the first years of school

The following sequence encourages younger students to explore a range of traditional stories and develop their own story-writing skills.

THE FROG PRINCE CONTINUED

Suitability	Years R–3
Duration	Eight sessions of 25-40 minutes each

Anticipated outcomes

Students will:

- explore a range of well-known and non-traditional fairy tales
- become familiar with the structure of fairy tales
- use their bodies to represent different fairy-tale characters and different moods, thoughts and feelings
- recognise that words on a page have meaning and can be read aloud in different ways to suggest different feelings
- share their own fairy tales orally and in writing
- understand the different phases of a fairy tale: orientation, complication, resolution
- work co-operatively in a small group.

Focus

Our feelings, moods and actions have an impact on those around us.

Session 1 As a whole group, revisit some well known fairy tales (eg *Snow White*, *Hansel and Gretel*, *The Frog Prince* and *Cinderella*). Have students choose their favourite character from a fairy tale and walk in role exploring this character. How do they walk? How do they walk when they are happy? Angry? Worried? Afraid? Ask students, in small groups, to take turns to look at each other and try to guess who is being depicted. Students conclude the session by drawing their character.

Session 2 Read *The Frog Prince Continued* to the point when the prince runs off into the forest to find a witch to turn him back into a frog. Discuss the text, the characters, and the situation. Students sculpt each other as either the Frog Prince or the Frog Princess. Tap in to the sculptures and ask the characters how they are feeling. Then have students paint the character they have depicted and add a thought or speech bubble expressing the character's feelings at a particular point in the story. They could list the characteristics of their character around their painting.

Session 3 Read the next section of the story until the fairy godmother turns the Frog Prince into a carriage. Identify the various fairy tales represented along the way. In small groups, students decide what happens next and share these possibilities with the class. Students can illustrate these alternative endings.

Session 4 Have small groups of students work in character to present a critical moment in the story as a freeze frame. As a class, view all the critical moments. Tap in at various points to find out how the characters are feeling. Record the still images with a digital camera; the students can add captions later.

Session 5 Build on students' motivation to reread a whole range of fairy tales and discuss the similarities of structure.

Sessions 6–8 Support pairs of students to plan and then write their own fairy tales. This should include the planning of characterisation, setting and sequencing, using frameworks that you provide (see the examples opposite). Those who need your help to scribe their stories could complete their illustrations first. If possible, arrange for upper-primary 'buddies' to word-process the stories, which can be published when final illustrations are completed. The students could then share their published fairy tales with other classes.

A Year 1 student's speech bubble after depicting the Frog Princess and tapping in to her feelings during a session exploring *The Frog Prince*

beyond the script

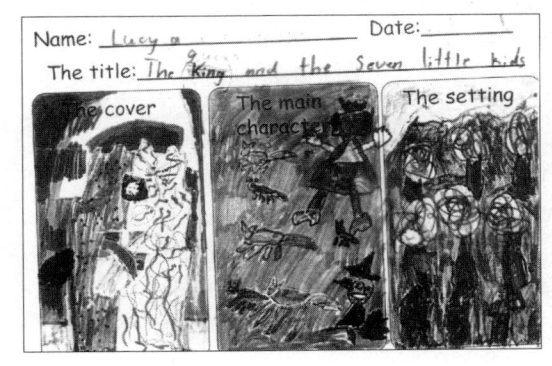

Student plans for written fairy tales, using teacher-supplied frameworks

Where to find further support

- Australian Storytelling Guild
  PO Box 76, Pendle Hill NSW 2145
  www.home.aone.net.au/stories/

- Teaching and Learning for Peace Foundation
  www.tlpeace.org.au

References and sources

Aylwin, A (1990) 'Telling and Retelling' in *Storytelling*. Inner London Education Authority. London.

Colwell, E (1991) *Storytelling*. Thimble, Stroud.

Cusworth, R (1995) 'The Framing of Educational Knowledge through Newstime in Junior Primary Classrooms'. Unpublished PhD, University of Sydney.

Egan, K (2003) 'Start with What the Student Knows or with What the Student Can Imagine?' *Phi Delta Kappan*. February.

Fox, C (1983) 'Talking Like a Book.' In Meek, M (ed.), *Opening Moves*. The Bedford Way Papers No. 17, University of London, London.

Fox, C (1993) *At the Very Edge of the Forest*. Cassell, London.

Hardy, B (1975) *Tellers and Listeners*. Athone Press, London.

Lowe, K (2002) *What's the Story? Making Meaning in Primary Classrooms*. Primary English Teaching Association, Sydney.

Martin, J & Rothery, J (1982) *Writing Project Report Working Papers in Linguisitics* No.2. University of Sydney, Sydney.

Scieszka, J (1991).*The Frog Prince Continued*. Viking, London.

Chapter Nine

Readers' theatre

Readers' theatre is a way of working collaboratively in order to interpret a story and present that interpretation to an audience. It is not only about reading, or only about talking, but brings together multiple modes in the dramatic form of group story-telling. Students use their voices to explore different readings of the same words, and they understand that all readers bring past experiences to the meanings they make from texts. It provides a bridge between choral reading and a fully staged performance.

Why readers' theatre?

There are many reasons for using readers' theatre in your classroom. Some important ones are discussed in what follows.

Building confidence in oral reading

Young and inexperienced readers are often asked to read aloud from the very first year of schooling so that their teachers can ascertain what strategies they're using. While it's sometimes necessary to ask students to read aloud for diagnostic reasons, it's imperative that you find ways to help them develop confidence about doing so. Readers' theatre can give them that confidence, and it helps them to practise their skills in a meaningful context.

Developing co-operative learning skills

Because students work together on how to read the script, they will need to share and discuss what a particular text means to them, who will read what, which sound effects will be most effective, and how they should arrange themselves to do the reading. Later, during the scripting process itself, they will need to reconcile differing interpretations to produce a script. Working co-operatively to unpack the meaning(s) of a text can be one of the best ways to demonstrate that everyone brings their own prior experiences to anything they read, and that there is no 'right' way to interpret a text.

Developing visual memory

Fundamentally, readers' theatre is about reading a script to an audience. Even though the script may have become very familiar through rehearsing, the reader still has it available for reference during performance. Readers' theatre is therefore useful for students whose visual memory isn't well developed — students who, for example, would find it difficult to learn a script by heart.

Supporting script-writing

There is great educational value in the process of developing a script from a narrative, giving thought to what is needed (and what isn't) for a group story-telling. Transforming a narrative text into a script gives students a scaffold for script-writing and, later, the editing process. It's much better for your students to create their own scripts, developed from an appropriate text, than to use books of ready-made scripts. The process also reflects the highly valued real-life role of screenplay adaptation — translating a narrative into a film script.

Exploring the role of narrator

Readers' theatre helps to develop students' understanding of the role of the storyteller and the narrator. Where an author has employed multiple voices in relating a story (like Libby Gleeson in *Dodger*), scripting for oral reading foregrounds the use of different perspectives and opens up discussion of this technique.

Focusing on voice

Movement, mime and still image (discussed in Chapter 3) allow students to focus on what they can communicate with their bodies using 'expressive silence'. By contrast, readers' theatre enables them to concentrate on the elements of voice that carry meaning — for example, accelerating and raising the pitch to suggest excitement. Readers' theatre has been called 'theatre of the mind' because voice — reinforced by facial expression and simple gestures — can often generate deeper and more powerful audience responses than full-blown theatre productions supported by 'bells and whistles'.

Increasing enjoyment

Underpinning all of the reasons given above is the fact that readers' theatre is a tremendous amount of fun. Students tend to learn most effectively if their learning experience is engaging and enjoyable. In addition, readers' theatre helps students to develop a sense of audience. As one child commented: *It helps you not be so shy in front of an audience and it feels like you are in the book.* It makes a good beginning for learning performance and presentation skills, and it doesn't involve the teacher in time-consuming costuming and stage choreography.

How to select a literary text to develop into a script

Choose an authentic literary text that you've been using for close study, and that the students have enjoyed. It must have literary merit, lend itself to scripting, and be a suitable length for the group. A picture-book text often provides a useful starting point for those unfamiliar with the process. Even when working with older students, it will be helpful to start with a picture book that you have shared together. For students who are beginning schooling, a text with lots of repetition is suitable. *Farmer Duck* (Waddell & Oxenbury, 1991) provides an excellent starting point for emerging readers; the duck only ever says *Quack!* but students can use their voices to indicate its growing exhaustion as it does more and more work around the farm. The other animals need to demonstrate their growing concern for the duck with their various moos, baas and clucks. Similarly, the farmer always asks: *How goes the work?*.

If you're using a chapter book, be careful to select an extract that lends itself to readers' theatre. A series of excerpts from a longer text, linked by narrative, also works well — as does poetry (see, for example, Alan Ahlberg's poetry collections). Narrative poems like *The Highwayman* can also be effective. Part of a script developed from the traditional American poem *The Hairy Toe* appears below.

Storyteller 1:	There was once an old lady went out to pick beans
Storyteller 2:	And she found a hairy toe.
Storyteller 3:	She took the hairy toe home with her
Storyteller 4:	And that night when she went to bed
Storyteller 1:	The wind began to
Wind:	MOAN
	GROAN
Storyteller 2:	Away off in the distance she seemed to hear a voice saying
Voice:	Who's got my hair-ry toe? Who's got my hair-ry toe?

Texts rich in dialogue often translate well into scripts because they come across more powerfully when their distinctive voices can be divided among a team of people. Some texts that use third-person narration can also be effective if they're divided among a number of storytellers. The opening of Ted Hughes' (1968) *The Iron Man*, for example, is very graphic when read by a number of storytellers because it turns on an echoing, question/answer device (even though it's not written as dialogue). The opening page was scripted by a group of 5/6 students thus:

Storyteller 1:	The Iron Man came to the top of the cliff.
Storyteller 2:	How far had he walked?
Storyteller 3:	Nobody knows.
Storyteller 4:	Where had he come from?
Storyteller 1:	Nobody knows.
Storyteller 2:	How was he made?
Storyteller 3:	Nobody knows.
Storyteller 4:	Taller than a house,
Storyteller 1:	the Iron Man stood at the top of the cliff,
Storyteller 2:	on the very brink,
Storyteller 3:	in the darkness.

Similarly, *Where the Wild Things Are* (Sendak, 1962) lends itself to multiple storytellers — only a group of children with percussion instruments can best create the wild, cacophonous rumpus effectively.

If you're going to adapt a copyrighted literary text for readers' theatre and take it through to performance before an invited audience, it's vital to seek permission from the publisher. Any script must acknowledge the source text and author at the beginning.

Initially, you'll have to take the lead in producing scripts but, in time, students will learn to do their own scripting (there's an example at the end of this chapter). Ensure that scripts include a number of characters and divide any narrative passages between several storytellers. If one reader has three paragraphs without a break, the whole point of multiple story-telling will be lost, and the other readers and audience may all lose interest.

Starting with readers' theatre

Understanding the concept

It's really quite difficult for students to understand what's meant by readers' theatre without having the opportunity to see it. If you're introducing it for the first time, it's a good idea to ask a small number of students to work with you beforehand so that they can model the concept to the whole class. Alternatively, ask an older group of students to model it, arrange for staff members to perform a script at an assembly, or use a video to demonstrate the process.

Developing familiarity with the script

Once your script is available in multiple copies, have students read it in pairs around the whole class. Using pairs initially avoids any student being put on the spot. Because you have been using the story for close study, students will be familiar with the words and the meaning of the story. Talk explicitly about using the voice to emphasise important elements in the story. Model some lines from the script, demonstrating how an emphasis on selected words can completely change the meaning. Depending on the age and experience of your class, you might demonstrate this by writing some lines on the board and underlining those which you are emphasising.

Sharing the script in small groups

Divide the class into small groups and allocate parts within each. Initially, ask the groups to read around together and consider how the script should be treated — how it might be read to convey different meanings. Margery Hertzberg (2000) has created a worksheet to help students think critically about their scripting decisions.

Readers' theatre instructions

First, just practise reading the script together.

As you continue to practise, think about the aspects below and, as a group, decide on:

Verbal expression: How will you speak your part?

tone (e.g. happy/sad)

volume (e.g. loudly/softly)

pace (e.g. quickly/slowly)

Body language

facial expressions

hand and other body gestures

Position: In readers' theatre you do not move very much, and you face the audience.

Where will you stand or sit?

Will you alter your position at times?

Sound effects: Do you want to use:

instruments?

body percussion?

Students can highlight their character's part in their script, which can be glued into a folder with the character drawn on the front. In addition, they can underline words that require particular emphasis in their oral reading. They can also think about a symbolic piece of costuming or a prop that will distinguish them from the other readers; for example, the three Billy Goats Gruff could have different-sized folders. Students should practise their reading on a number of occasions, perhaps underlining words that need special emphasis. At this point you may wish to form expert groups of characters reading the same part. They can discuss the way they interpret various lines. For example, all those reading Father Bear in *Peace at Last* can compare and contrast how they will use their voice to demonstrate growing frustration in the repetitive *I can't stand this* as the night noises in the house prevent him from falling asleep. Or how might they repeat the Bunyip's *What am I? What am I? What am I?* in Jenny Wagner's *Bunyip of Berkeley Creek* (1977) over and over in a way that indicates increasing despair?

Refining the reading of the script

Blocking

Once students feel confident with the reading of their script, encourage them to think about how they might arrange themselves on the stage at different levels in front of an audience. For example, one group of students reading Kellogg's *Chicken Little* (1988) had every character except Chicken Little stand on a chair.

Sound effects

Ask the groups to consider whether percussion instruments or body percussion might be used to add emphasis at particular points, or whether other musical sounds might be more appropriate. For instance, Libby Gleeson's *The Princess and the Perfect Dish* (1995) is enhanced by the sounding of a melody each time the princess tastes the delicious fruit; Steven Kellogg's *Chicken Little* benefits from sound effects indicating that an acorn has fallen from the sky or the helicopter has come crashing down on the fox. Students can note any music or sound effects in their scripts.

Performing

You won't necessarily wish to take every reading of a readers' theatre script to full performance. Nevertheless, there will be times when students who've had a really wonderful time with a script want to perform it. Such performances can be a fitting culmination for them — and for the rest of the class, or the class next door, or a whole-school assembly. If it's decided to go this way, the readers will need some extra rehearsal time. For a performance, students can wear a symbolic piece of costume or carry a prop that helps to define who they are. They will hold the script in their hands but focus their gaze at a mid-point above the heads of the audience. In this form of theatre, the actors are not playing to each other but to the audience. They concentrate on using voice, face and gesture to create the story in the minds of their listeners.

Towards independent scripting

Once students have absorbed the process from your modelling, they can be given opportunities to script for themselves (though they won't become entirely competent overnight). With older students, you might find that a novel you've chosen for close study contains a passage that lends itself to multiple reading.

Libby Gleeson's *Eleanor, Elizabeth* opens with the children in the car going to their new house. Eleanor is thinking about having left Brunswick Heads for a dry and dusty country town, how hot it's going to be, and how she's going to miss her friends. At the same time she and her brother are playing *I Spy*. This part of the text really lends itself to being read by a number of voices. However, it's also a passage that students may need help with. There's an ongoing inner voice interwoven with lots of dialogue, and less experienced readers may need to be shown what's happening, who's speaking when, and so on. It might be a good idea to begin by scripting a little bit yourself, and then give students the chance to develop the script themselves. How will they indicate Eleanor's inner thoughts and distinguish these from her spoken words? Some groups of students have represented Eleanor's thoughts with a voice read from off centre or even from off stage. Others have chosen to have most characters sitting, with a second child standing behind the seated Eleanor to deliver her thoughts.

The Shrinking of Treehorn (Heide, 1975) is particularly suited to readers moving from texts with heavy visual support to chapter books. At the beginning of the story, Treehorn starts to get smaller and smaller, but his mother doesn't notice or even hear his concerns — she's too busy thinking about why her cake didn't rise, or spring-cleaning the house. When she finally does notice, she blames her son. There are all sorts of delightful snatches of conversation through the book: for example, when Treehorn gets on the bus and the driver says he must be Treehorn's brother because he looks exactly the same but smaller; when he gets into trouble at school because he can't reach the bubbler; and when the principal interviews him for this misdemeanour. Small groups could script four or five of these excerpts. These scripts could then be linked by a few lines of jointly constructed narrative that summarise what's happened between each scene.

Turning an excerpt from a novel into a readers' theatre script makes students think about the role of the narrator (or narrators) in a text; about the presence of multiple voices; about the differences between spoken and written language; and about the power of their own voices to make meaning. Ideally, they should try adapting some of their own narrative writing.

It can also be rewarding to combine readers' theatre with other drama strategies. For instance, one group of students can read the script while another mimes the action or uses a series of still images to represent critical moments in the story.

An excellent text to help students get started with scripting is Lauren Child's *The Case of the Storybook Wolves* (2000). Child has represented different characters with different fonts and conveyed meanings with different font sizes etc. Working with groups of three or four, give each group a page of the text and ask them to decide how to script for multiple storytellers as well as Herb, the wolves etc. Each group can then share its page of script in sequence. Part of a script created in this way by a Year 3/4 group appears below.

> *Herb (stammering)*: I wouldn't eat me yet!
>
> *Big Wolf*: Why not?
>
> *Little Wolf*: Yes, why not?
>
> *Herb*: Ummmmm ... because little boys are for pudding. You have to start with starters, of course.
>
> *Big Wolf*: I didn't know that.

Herb: Really?

Storyteller 1: Herb felt a bit pleased with his own craftiness.

Herb: I thought everybody knew that.

Little Wolf: Oh, I knew that.

Big Wolf: No you did not.

Storyteller 2: He was slightly less fierce than before.

References and sources

Ahlberg, A (1989) *Heard It in the Playground*. Viking, London.

Child, L (2000) *The Case of the Storybook Wolves*. Hodder, London.

Gleeson, L (1990) *Dodger*. Turton & Chambers, Victoria Park, WA.

Gleeson, L (1984) *Eleanor, Elizabeth*. Angus & Robertson, Sydney.

Gleeson, L (1995) *The Princess and the Perfect Dish*. Scholastic, Sydney.

Heide, F (1971) *The Shrinking of Treehorn*. Puffin, Harmondsworth.

Hertzberg, M (2000) 'How Does Educational Drama Enhance Children's Language and Literacy Development?'. Unpublished doctoral thesis. University of Western Sydney.

Hughes, T (1968) *The Iron Man*. Faber & Faber, London.

Kellogg, S (1988) *Chicken Little*. Arrow Books, London.

Murphy J (1980). *Peace at Last*. Picture Puffin, Harmondsworth.

Sendak, M (1962) *Where the Wild Things Are*. Harper & Rowe, London.

Waddell, M & Oxenbury, H (1991) *Farmer Duck*. Walker, Loon.

Wagner, J (1977) *The Bunyip of Berkeley's Creek*. Picture Puffin, Harmondsworth.

CHAPTER TEN

Drama when English is an additional language

MARGERY HERTZBERG

Most English as an additional language (EAL) learners in our schools have attained basic English competency and may not receive specialist English-language teacher assistance. This chapter demonstrates how drama can be used to enhance these students' language and literacy skills in mainstream classes.

Many students report anecdotally that drama assists their English development (Hertzberg, 2000). The comments below reveal the thoughts of two EAL students who have moved beyond the beginning stage of learning English.

> When you have to use your imagination, you can think up better ideas ...
> so when you think, you must be learning more English.
>
> It helps you communicate your thoughts because you can feel the situation,
> and you have more opinions because you take on that role.

The common thread in these remarks is the demand that drama places on participants to preformulate ideas, as inner speech, that must be communicated externally. Put another way, drama offers students like these 'a role to speak'. 'Role', in this sense, doesn't mean the conventional character role that's assumed in the simulated role-plays that are common practice in second-language teaching. Usually, simulated role-plays are set up *by* teachers *for* students, in order to practise particular language functions and structures. For instance, so that students can practise requesting, a teacher might establish a scenario in which students simulate ordering at a restaurant. However, the process of *enactment* (a concept explained earlier in this book) gives students the 'role to speak' in sustained conversations. It operates not just at the performing stage, but also in the preparatory and reflective stages. The process gives students an opportunity to debate and challenge their own thoughts and the thoughts of others within a fictional context. Students are often more prepared to take risks. As one student in interview said: "I like it [drama] 'cause you can say things that are you, but nobody has to know because you are acting someone else".

Taking risks is critical for learning. Yet for many EAL students, talking through issues and ideas in more traditional class activities can be threatening and inhibiting. Furthermore, in many class discussions, EAL students may not have as many opportunities to say what they think because it takes them longer to articulate their inner thoughts, by which time other students have spoken for them. Yet talking and listening are essential components in any lesson for EAL students.

When students are beginning to learn English, talking and listening activities form the basis for teaching. With a crowded curriculum to address, though, there is pressure to rush through talking and listening activities — and onto the reading and writing components — once students have attained proficiency in everyday English. This presents a threat to learning. Many such students continue to lack the academic language of school, and need more opportunities to hear and use these academic registers before, and in conjunction with, reading and writing.

Language needs of EAL students beyond the beginning stage

Learning conversational language takes about two years. However, learning the language necessary for academic learning takes at least 5–7 years (Cummins, 2000). Some learners never achieve this level — *not* because they have learning difficulties, but because they haven't been given sufficient opportunities to practise the higher-order language functions and structures so necessary for academic achievement. Some of these language functions are, for example, informing, deducing, reflecting, analysing, inferring, speculating, synthesising, solving problems, justifying/persuading, comparing and evaluating. This could be one of the reasons that many EAL students remain 'stabilised' or 'fossilised' — stuck at a conversational stage of English development.

Drama is well placed to develop the above language functions, not just because it involves talking and listening, but because of the *type* of talking and listening that takes place. A useful analogy is the family dinner-table debate. In this situation, participants discuss, for instance, current issues. In so doing, they use many higher-order language functions. Of course bilingual children have these experiences, too, but not necessarily in English. That's why similar opportunities need to be planned explicitly in classrooms. This presents a challenge for you as a teacher within an institutional setting, because it's often difficult to practise the language of the real world in plausible and engaging contexts. Drama is a useful ally in meeting this challenge. While it doesn't offer reality, it offers life-like contexts and demands. In doing so, it can fulfil many of the major principles underpinning EAL theory, as the following table demonstrates.

Table 11.1: Relationship between selected principles of second-language acquisition and educational drama

Principle of second-language acquisition	Feature of educational drama
Based on a social view of learning: students and teachers establish and engage in collaborative and active learning environments Communication occurs in interaction with others	A collaborative art form; active learning is central Small-group work rather than teacher instruction
Talking, listening, reading and writing should not be artificially segmented	Enactment often draws on all strands of English

Principle of second-language acquisition	Feature of educational drama
A range of registers along the spoken-mode continuum (from most spoken-like to most written-like) are practised	Drama forms range from spontaneous improvisation to scripted plays; so, too, do the variety of modes within a specific drama form
Receptive language (what the student understands) usually precedes expressive language (what the student can say), but cognitive challenge must be maintained, along with contextual support	Non-verbal language – gesture, space, levels, movement – assists communication of understanding Dramatic contexts provide opportunities to participate in challenging and age-appropriate activities, even if oral English is insufficiently developed or confidence is lacking
Language learnt through use in meaningful contexts Must be opportunities for purposeful talk Structured opportunities for speakers to clarify meaning through negotiating and rewording	Participants listen to others and use language to clarify meaning, negotiate content – especially in the preparation and rehearsal stages
Recognition that language use depends on the context of the situation	Variety of fictional contexts enables participants to practise or experience a range of language registers not easily achieved in conventional schooling contexts

Principle of second-language acquisition	Feature of educational drama
Requires 'field-building' – connecting prior knowledge and experience to new learning	Based on students' own ideas rather than prescribed texts Pre-texts with familiar issues can be used to elicit both deeper meaning and new learning
Outer speech or external dialogue with others assists inner speech or abstract thinking — essential for problem-solving and independent thinking	Demands of dialogue – formulation of responses – assist inner speech Some dramatic strategies support inner speech directly, eg thought tunnel, thought-tapping, voice collage
Language use must be scaffolded with planned and contingent teacher support	Initial dramatic framework and structures planned by the teacher support students to acquire new skills/ideas and transfer these to other situations Some dramatic strategies such as hot-seating and drama-circle discussion enable the teacher and more capable students to model and extend language use

Drama plans

Each of the three drama plans that follow incorporate some of the features highlighted in the table above. The talking and listening components, prior to reading and writing, are common to all plans.

PLAN 1

Story drama for *The Very Hungry Caterpillar*

Synopsis

This plan is based around a story suitable for students in the first year of schooling — an imaginative story about the life cycle of caterpillars that also reinforces concepts such as the days of the week and the number sequence 1–10. If you are just beginning to implement drama, this type of 'story drama' is an easy way in. In essence, someone reads a story while the group enacts it. It can be applied to any story with a time sequence and one main character. This plan integrates drama, literature and science, focusing on using the language of drama to retell a story and then innovate on this text to write a new story.

Classroom organisation and management

This activity can be done easily in a classroom. You may need to move some tables to create enough space.

You are directed to tap a tambourine at certain points. This device is aimed at stopping activity while signifying an end to part of the story. Note that each final activity ends with a sleep or a rest, designed to calm participants down.

1. Building the field: Before reading the book

Class discussion
Ascertain students' prior knowledge, including vocabulary. Talk about caterpillars and their life cycle.

Mime
Ask students to imagine that they are each of the things listed opposite, and to represent each by miming.

- Caterpillar in an egg
- Caterpillar hatching from the egg
- Caterpillar growing bigger
- Caterpillar with a stomach ache because it has eaten too much
- Caterpillar in a cocoon
- Caterpillar nibbling its way out of the end of the cocoon
- Butterfly
- Butterfly landing on a flower and sipping nectar
- Butterfly sleeping

2. Reading the story

Read *The Very Hungry Caterpillar* (Carle, 1970) as the students listen.

Discuss the fact that the story is fictional and, as such, is not scientifically accurate, although the cycle is correct.

3. Dramatising the reading

Narration and mime

Read the story again. This time, each student becomes the caterpillar and acts out the events as you read.

Tap the tambourine at the end of each story event to freeze the action before going onto the next event.

While the story ends with the butterfly flying, consider finishing your reading with the butterfly finding a flower to land on and sipping nectar before finding a leaf on which to sleep as a calming effect.

4. Writing based on this book

Innovating on a text

Support the joint construction of a narrative also based on the idea of a life cycle, but using students' own character, setting and action suggestions.> Once the story-drafting is complete, dramatise the new story's events as above.

> *PETA's monograph* The Wishing Crystal: Joint Construction in the Junior-primary Classroom *(Parkin, 2003) provides an excellent basis for establishing and reflecting upon this activity.*

Example

The extract below is the first part of a story jointly constructed early in Term 2 with eight children from a Kindergarten/Year 1 class that had an 80% EAL enrolment. At the time, the students were studying the life cycle of frogs. This small group worked with the EAL teacher. They reread *The Very Hungry Caterpillar* and then, innovating on this story's structure, wrote a story about a tadpole. Their story concludes with the frog lying on a rock and eating mosquitoes and flies to keep the owners of the pond happy.

> In the light of the moon a little egg lay on the surface of the water. >
>
> One Sunday morning the warm sun came up and pop out of the egg hatched a tiny and very hungry tadpole.
>
> She swam around the fishpond looking for food.
>
> On Monday she ate one rotten apple core, but she was still hungry.
>
> On Tuesday she nibbled >> on two sandwich crusts, but she was still hungry.
>
> On Wednesday she nibbled on three orange peels, but she was still hungry ...

> \> An example of introducing scientific language. In the first draft, 'on top of the water' was provided and accepted. This was modified, with explanation, in the final copy.

> \>\> An example of refinement during the drafting process. Originally, 'ate' was used throughout. In the second draft, 'nibbled' was offered by a student who thought 'ate' was being used too repetitively.

PLAN 2

Using pictures as a drama stimulus

This drama plan is suitable for students in the middle-primary years. It was developed to enhance students' skills in writing a literary description. After the lesson, a student said she was going to pretend to do drama during the state-wide literacy test (where students are sometimes presented with a stimulus photo and asked to write a literary description) because "if I pretend that I'm doing drama — then I'll use my imagination and come up with some good ideas".

1. Introducing the picture

Show students a photo of a dog. The weekend newspaper magazines often have suitably large pictures. Introduce the dog. For example: "This is Bella. She is very gentle and loves going for walks in her local park."

2. Building the field

Ask the students to describe a park they like going to, activities that take place in the park, and so forth.

3. Collective mapping

Have students develop the fictional park where Bella goes for walks, encouraging them to add as many features as possible.

4. Role development

Ask the students to imagine they are one of the people that Bella meets at the park on her daily walk. Provide these guiding questions:

- Who are you?
- How do you know Bella?
- Where are you in the park?
- What are you doing in the park?

5. Still image

Ask students, in role, to create a still image of themselves in the park.

6. Writing

Have students draw a rough sketch of their character in their drama journals, and write words around the sketch to describe their character in terms of relationship to Bella, personality, hobbies and so forth.

7. Questioning in role (Hot-seating)

Ask a volunteer to describe her or his character briefly to the class. Class members then ask more questions to help develop this character.

Now form students into groups of four and continue the questioning-in-role activity so that all students have a turn.

8. Writing

Have students return to their journals and write the new information they have about their character in point form. They then construct their notes into a prose passage.

Request a volunteer to share a rough draft with the class. Use this as a model to discuss the language structures and features of literary descriptions. This will include, for example, the predominant use of present simple tense, types of personal pronouns, noun groups and so forth.> Students then return to their work and redraft.

> *For additional information, refer to PETA books such as* A Grammar Companion for Primary Teachers *(Derewianka, 1998) and* Writing Links *(Love & Rushton, 2000).*

Further possibilities

This drama activity can provide an introductory framework for playbuilding (see Chapter 7). To begin, you might read the humorous poem *The Dog Who Wouldn't Come* (Ahlberg, (1997), which students might perform as a choral reading. The students could then develop a drama (perhaps using this poem as a ritual) that might explore issues such as the responsibilities involved in caring for pets, or the importance of pets as companions.

PLAN 3

Drama program for *Painted Words, Spoken Memories*

Synopsis

Cross-cultural themes feature in this picture book (Brandenburg, 1998). As with many picture books, it can be read on a variety of levels, making it suitable for all ages. It's about an immigrant girl (Mari) and her family. With no country names disclosed, the story universalises themes such as displacement, language and custom barriers. It begins with Mari entering school unable to speak English. At first, she tells her story through paintings, revealing impressions of her new environment and offering hints about her family's past. Then, in the second section, the story of Mari's family and community life is told in both words and pictures, illuminating the family's reasons for migrating.

For many EAL students, these concepts and issues are familiar, but the telling of the story is not confronting. It is neither moralistic nor pessimistic, and it is dedicated to "unsung teachers who change and enrich lives".

The following drama program takes about four hours and would ordinarily be completed in sessions over a week or two.

1. Building the field: Before reading the book

Individual still image

Have students stand in a large circle with their backs to the centre of the circle. Ask them to make a still image that captures the moment when they feel nervous about meeting a large group of new people. Alternatively, they might show their perception of this situation but in role as a new immigrant. Allow about five seconds for thinking and preparation. On the count of three, the students freeze their image.

Next, ask the students to make another still image that captures how they feel after one of this group is welcoming to them.

Note: This introductory exercise provides protection for students, respecting their right to anonymous thoughts and feelings. Facing outwards from the circle ensures that participants cannot see each other.

2. Reading the book

Read the book right through. Elicit the main themes and issues that are apparent to students at this point, e.g. English-language difficulties, bullying, poverty, war, safety and isolation. There's no need for a lengthy discussion at this stage — the drama activities will give *all* students an opportunity to express themselves.

3. Rereading the book

Form reading groups of three. At appropriate times during the day have these small groups read the book again. This environment will give students a better opportunity to engage with the meanings and impacts of the illustrations.

4. Responding to the first half (*Painted Words*)

Sculpting

Return to the beginning of book and reread up to the section where Mari shakes hands with the teacher.

Form the students into pairs. In each pair, one person sculpts the other to show how they think Mari might be feeling as she waves goodbye to her mother on the first day.

In a whole-group drama circle, ask one pair of students to volunteer to show their sculpture. The sculptor explains why s/he sculpted the other person to look as s/he does. Discuss the interpretation and hence issues about language barriers, customs and so forth.

This sculpting activity could be repeated to represent how the mother and/or teacher feels.

Voice collage (Soundscape)

Ask individuals to write one word that describes Mari's feelings. Then bring the words together by asking the whole group to perform a voice collage.

Again, this activity could be repeated to focus on the mother or the teacher. Suggest that students use a thesaurus to find new descriptive vocabulary. Words such as *petrified*, *tentative*, *hesitant* and *timid* might emerge.

Alternatively, you might suggest that half the class express Mari's feelings and the other half express the teacher or mother's feelings.

Still image and thought-tracking

Form the students into groups of three. Ask the groups to view the picture that shows Danny bullying Mari as Kristen watches. Students assume the roles of Mari, Danny or Kristin. Ask each group to make a still image of this scene. Then tap each character in turn, asking her/him to verbalise their thoughts at this moment.

Note: The students might want to debate the various interpretations of Kristen. Is she detached or concerned?

Role walk

Read the section: "We have a great deal to talk about," said Mr Petrie. "Let our ideas begin."

Form the students into a drama circle. Ask them to close their eyes and imagine how Mari feels about being bullied. Then ask all students, in role as Mari, to stand and walk slowly around the circle. While walking, students think of a word to describe how they (as Mari) feel when Patrick is bullying her. When tapped on the shoulder, they say this word. Note, however, that participants can choose to remain silent by saying pass.

Reform the drama circle and discuss Mari's feelings, and the effect of bullying on her. You might also return to the page that shows Patrick taking building blocks from another group of children. Guide the discussion to address why people bully, its effects, what bystanders can do, and so forth.

Once again, this activity could be repeated to investigate the feelings of Kristen, Patrick and/or Rachel.

Conscience alley

Return to final page of the *Painted Words* section, where Mari successfully talks to her paintings at news time. Ask one person to volunteer to be Mari. Form the rest of the group into two lines. As Mari walks between the lines, ask each person to say how they feel, or what they think, about her illustrated story, as well as her ability to articulate it. They should say something to affirm Mari's actions.

5. Responding to the second half (*Spoken Memories*)

Questioning in role (Hot-seating)

Reread the pages where Uncle Theo reads a letter from Mari's father. (*Note that the details of the letter aren't provided in the story itself.*)

Ask one person to take on the role of the father (or take it on yourself). The rest of the class questions the father to establish his character and experiences as an immigrant. Allow around three minutes for students to formulate their questions.

As a whole group, retrace the main information provided above to aid students in the subsequent writing activity. As well, discuss the issues that arise, e.g. feelings of loneliness and isolation, learning about different customs and food, language difficulties, and happy or funny situations.

Still image

Ask all students to assume the role of the father and portray an event/moment/situation revealed in the questioning-in-role activity.

Writing in role

Ask all students, in role as the father, to write a letter back home, telling the family his news.

Narrating an image

Make an overhead transparency of the picture showing Uncle Theo reading the letter. While the whole group views the picture, one student reads their letter from the back of the room.

Alternatively, this activity could be done in groups of five. Each group interprets the illustration as a still image, while the 'uncle' reads one of the group's letters.

Still image

Ask students, in groups of four, to depict a future moment in this family's life. The moment might be anything from two to twenty years or more hence. Mari should be part of the depiction, and the moment should depict an important event for this family.

Build in a dramatic constraint: explain that the still image needs to show a problem that is occurring. Something is not quite right or unexpected, or someone is resisting. (You might stipulate that nobody can die, to move the interpretation away from 'cops-and-robbers' action.) To help students plan their scene, use the framework questions who, what, where, why, how.

Note: You might want to provide some objects to aid in developing ideas. The objects could help to clarify the dramatic focus and/or represent a key theme. Some examples include: Australian flag, photo frame, playing cards, camera, red scarf, paintbrush, sparkler, box of chocolates, binoculars.

Tap each person consecutively on the shoulder, asking each to give voice to her or his thoughts in this moment.

Improvisation

Build on the still image with a further challenge. Ask the groups to consider the minutes leading up to their frozen scene. Challenge them to improvise the interactions that might have occurred — to flesh out the story to this point.

Note: This is a good strategy for students new to drama because they already have the ending, which is often the most difficult part to plan. You might want to take photos of these still images and invite students to write accompanying prose. In this way, the students, too, may be authors of picture books!

Where to now?

The above program is a good starting point towards sensitising and debating issues around cultural and linguistic diversity. Reading *Boy Overboard* (Gleitzman, 2002), which explores the experiences of Afghani refugees, is a logical extension. Many drama strategies suggested throughout this book fit well with that text. Making readers' theatre scripts is ideal, as they help to capture the tension that makes the book so poignant.

Another potential follow-up is *NIPS X1* (Starke, 2000). In this book, the protagonist — Australian-born Lan, who is of Vietnamese descent — challenges the school principal, who adheres to the practice of celebrating Australia's cultural diversity by just having the annual multicultural day. Idiom and colloquial language make this book, but these forms of expression can pass by EAL students and weaken their understanding and engagement. For example, as the principal pontificates at the school assembly about the importance of multicultural day, Lan raises his hand and asks if there will be Australian food, like lamingtons. The question causes the principal to give "a snort that made the vigorous hairs sprouting from his nostrils quiver" (p 7). Not only do students enjoy miming or sculpting this scene, but when they do, they're required to analyse the construction of this noun group to convey the image. Such drama activity is considerably more beneficial than whole-class discussions for the few, or individual worksheets.

It's fair to acknowledge that drama takes longer than some other activities, and you should always consider whether there are quicker and more efficient ways for students to achieve a particular learning outcome. Let's leave the last word to an EAL teacher who is discussing her drama program around another book that is great for drama— *I Am Jack* (Gervay, 2000). Could her program's aims have been achieved more efficiently?

> No. No way. I don't think so. Yes, it's much longer than giving a very expository lesson and saying "OK, we've read this passage and now I want you to go away and write your opinion about Jack, and why you think he finds it difficult to talk to his Mum". Or "OK, now let's look at how the author has used direct and indirect speech" and then have a teacher-directed question time. But drama — OK, it did take longer — but all the kids are involved and I really think they are learning more and more deeply, and that's for me what quality teaching is about. It's not how long or short the lesson is that matters — it's whether they are learning

anything substantial. Which comes back to the point I made about risk-taking earlier [in this interview]. I said many kids here don't like to take risks. They don't want to do anything wrong. They are so scared of getting it wrong. They would rather just do tick-and-flick stencils, but drama takes them outside that box, out of that comfort zone, and they have to really think about the content, which leads to deeper understanding.

References and sources

Ahlberg, A (1997) *The Mysteries of Zigomar*. Walker Books, London.

Brandenburg, A (1998) *Painted Words, Spoken Memories*. Greenwillow Books, New York.

Carle, E (1970) *The Very Hungry Caterpillar*. Puffin Books, UK.

Cummins, J (2000) *Language, Power and Pedagogy: Bilingual Children in the Crossfire*. Multilingual Matters, Clevedon, UK.

Derewianka, B (1998) *A Grammar Companion for Primary Teachers*. Primary English Teaching Association, Sydney.

Gervay, S (2000) *I Am Jack*. Angus & Robertson, Sydney.

Gleitzman, M (2002) *Boy Overboard*. Puffin, Melbourne.

Hertzberg, M (2000) 'How Does Educational Drama Enhance Children's Language and Literacy Development?'. Unpublished doctoral dissertation. University of Western Sydney.

Love, C & Rushton, K (2000) *Writing Links: Grammar in Studies of Society and Environment*. Primary English Teaching Association, Sydney.

Parkin, B (2003) 'The Wishing Crystal: Joint Construction in the Junior-primary Classroom'. *PEN* 138. Primary English Teaching Association, Sydney.

Starke, R (2000) *NIPS XI*. Lothian Books, Melbourne.

CHAPTER ELEVEN

Evaluation and assessment

Outcomes-based education has given rise to some important issues for the evaluation and assessment of drama. Teachers sometimes wrongly believe that outcomes-based education demands that they observe and measure behavioural changes in their students at the end of each lesson or unit. At worst, this sort of attitude leads to a focus on the mastery of technical skills and a failure to appreciate the less observable but more important contributions that drama (and the arts more generally) can make to learning (see Chapter 5).

Drama can develop critical-thinking and literacy skills that are not so easy to measure. It can bring about shifts in perspective. It can sow seeds for the making of meaning which won't necessarily germinate at the site of the experience, but may grow and bear fruit much later.

Defining terms

Evaluation

At the core, *evaluation* involves making a judgement about someone or something. However, as Kemmis and Stake (1988) have pointed out, judgements are not absolute. They are always made "in a context of understanding shaped by personal biographies, by culture and by ideology" (p 9). In a drama experience, as in any other learning context, you will often make professional judgements about your students' involvement and responses. These judgements may feel intuitive but, as Ben Shahn observed (Best, 1980:124):

> Intuition in art is actually the result of prolonged tuition. The so-called innocent eye does not exist. The eye at birth cannot perceive at all, and it is only through training that it learns to recognise what it sees.

You do need to trust your 'intuitive' judgements — built up over years of professional and personal experience — when you're observing what your students are learning through drama.

John Thompson (1991) argues that as teachers gain experience in teaching drama, they become *connoisseurs*, able to lead their students to the appreciation of its complexity. They "know what to look for, are able to recognise skill, form and creativity" (p 80). Then they are able to use their connoisseur's eye to make evaluations that will affect further decisions about the pacing and direction of learning experiences.

Assessment

Assessment is a term often used to refer to appraising or measuring performance. As noted above, some drama skills and understandings are easy to measure (e.g. a student's ability to write in role), while others are less easily assessed, because they may not be observable for some time. While some thoughts and feelings about ageing/dependence and human relationships/interdependence can be demonstrated now, students who've explored the notion of getting old through enacting Miss Nancy in *Wilfred Gordon Macdonald Partridge* (Margaret Wild & Julie Vivas), or Hannah's grandpa in Libby Gleeson's *Hannah and the Tomorrow Room*, may not be able to express the sophistication of their understandings in any tangible way until they have to decide on nursing-home care for a parent many years later. One teacher only learnt of the impact of drama activities used to explore Anthony Browne's *Piggybook* when some parents reported a growing willingness to share the housekeeping chores at home. Learning in every Key Learning Area has residual, long-term outcomes that can't always be assessed straight away.

The most useful form of assessment for K–6 drama is *formative* rather than *summative*. That is, you will usually rely on day-to-day value judgements to pinpoint areas that require further development. Often the term 'assessment' is equated with a numerical mark but, as pointed out by Rowntree (cited in Thompson 1991:76), assessment occurs

> ... whenever one person, in some kind of interaction, direct or indirect, with another, is conscious of obtaining and interpreting information about the knowledge and understanding, or abilities and attitudes of that other person. To some extent it is an attempt to know that person.

Principles of evaluation and assessment in drama

- Assessment and evaluation must always acknowledge the *subjective* nature of the judgement being made, and the purpose of the judgement. However, as an adult experienced in the teaching of drama, you can apply your appreciation of the art form to your judgements.
- As much information should be gathered from as many perspectives as possible (including your students').
- Student self-evaluation strategies can be very rewarding and informative.
- Providing opportunities to talk, draw and write about drama experiences provides further evidence of, and further insights into, students' understandings.
- Not every piece of work need be assessed.
- Criteria for assessment in drama need to be developed and discussed with students, so that they understand the purpose(s) of assessment activities. For example, if you want students to show their ability to work together in small groups, the criteria for demonstrating this ability need to be workshopped beforehand.
- Drama activities can often be used to assess student learning in other learning areas. In English, asking students to depict three critical moments in a story readily demonstrates their understanding of a text, especially if they are able to justify their choices. Similarly, writing in role (as exemplified over) can be a powerful indicator of a student's understanding of a character's perspective.
- Reflection is the most important component of evaluation and assessment.

> John's Point of view.
>
> I hope they don't take me away from my family and culture. I love these people and I don't want to leave them. I'm really scared and don't want the big man from welfare to recognise me they say that they'll be back, even if I'm with my mother for one more day, I'll be glad. If only I was as black as the others they would never have come for me.
>
> By Erin

An example of student writing in role

Tracking tools

Whole-class and small-group discussion

Discussion can take place during a drama experience or afterwards. Sometimes you may stop the drama at a certain point to discuss students' responses, other possibilities and so on; at other times you may find it better to wait until the end of the session. Small-group discussions can sometimes be more productive than whole-class ones: you can audiotape these or nominate a student in each group to provide a report.

Student journals

Students can use journals to reflect on their own learning and that of their peers. However, the whole process of journal-writing needs to be carefully scaffolded. If you are planning to read your students' journals, you need to negotiate this transparently with your class. It may be preferable to have them choose the entries they are willing to have you read.

Student comments on the best and worst aspects of drama sessions can be illuminating, as these examples show.

> People were doing their own thing and not paying attention. Most of us sounded too young to be adults in the story.

> This drama made me think of people on the streets and the things that happened to them.
>
> The drama was a total mess. Everyone was mucking up. I tried to be in role, but I really felt upset and angry because everyone was silly.
>
> It was fun. It feels good when you play someone else, and get to feel how your character would feel.

Journal entries like these can redirect the focus of your teaching. For example, one Year 5 teacher was able to adapt his lessons when he read:

> I felt bored. The hot-seating was OK, and the circle activities were fun but the rest [talking] was boring.

It was clear that he needed to build in more physical activity and give this particular student more space to express herself.

Teacher journals

You can keep your own record of your perceptions during or after drama sessions. Descriptive comments, follow-up suggestions and anecdotal accounts can all be included, and photos and videos can form a valuable supplement.

Portfolios

Each student can keep a scrapbook or folder containing photos, writing and drawing to record his or her development in drama, responses to performances viewed etc. Comments from parents and friends can also be included.

Written and graphic responses in or out of role

An excerpt from Agi's PMI inventory — listing the pluses, minuses and interesting aspects of removing so-called 'half-caste' indigenous children from their parents — appears over. She wrote this after her teacher had modelled the PMI approach while the class was using a range of drama strategies to explore Anthony Hill's *The Burnt Stick*. The inventory demonstrates how well she had grasped some very complex issues surrounding Australia's stolen generation.

Plus	Minus	Interesting
Sometimes 'half caste' children weren't included in all of the tribal customs. Would learn new skills.	Lose their knowledge of their indigenous culture. Taken away from mother and family and friends and sometimes didn't see them again.	Wouldn't be able to sleep under the stars anymore.

More conventional written responses can be equally valuable, as demonstrated in these Year 5 comments on readers' theatre:

> When you read the script and act it feels that you are in the book and you feel really proud of yourself.

> I found readers' theatre interesting 'cos it was fun. It makes you not be so shy in front of an audience. I like when I read because it gives me a chance to use another accent. It's fun being someone else for a change.

> I like readers' theatre because if you want to read poems or act you have to improve how you say it.

Observation

Because it's difficult to be aware of individual progress, systematically observing a small number of students each week is also worthwhile. Alternatively, you could appoint students as observers, either of a group or (as critical friends) of just one peer.

Audio/Video recording

Photos and video recordings can provoke discussion of particular points amongst a whole class or within small groups. Audiotapes will help students and teacher to concentrate on the aural dimension, and are especially valuable for readers' theatre and puppetry. Some photos of the critical moments from *The Burnt Stick*, as chosen and depicted by Year 5 students, appear opposite.

Moments recorded from enactment of 'The Burnt Stick'

Questionnaires and rating scales

Students can be asked to respond to a series of questions, either in written form or orally. Younger students can draw their responses. Rating on a scale — from a very sad to a very happy face — is also feasible for younger students.

The after party: Celebrating success

One particular Year 6 group wrote a puppet play suitable for Kindergarten, based on a fairy story. They made sock puppets and a stage behind which the puppeteers hid themselves while one group member narrated the story. They performed their puppet play for a class of Kindergarten/Reception students who watched wide-eyed and laughed out loud at the jokes.

At the end of the performance the puppeteers came out from behind the puppet stage and let the audience see and play with the puppets they had created.

Everyone then celebrated the performance with a party.

As well as giving the audience a good time, these students were helping to create a whole new of cohort of potential performers.

References and sources

Best, D (1980) *The Rationality of Feeling*. Falmer Press, London.

Browne, A (1990) *Piggybook*. Julia Macrae, London.

Gleeson, L (1999) *Hannah and the Tomorrow Room*. Penguin Books, Australia.

Hill, A (1994) *The Burnt Stick*. Viking, Melbourne.

Kemmis, S & Stake, R (1988) *Evaluating Curriculum*.
Deakin University Press, Geelong.

Thompson, J (1991) 'Assessing Drama: Allowing for Meaningful Interpretation'. In Hughes, J (ed.), *Drama in Education: The State of the Art*. Educational Drama Association, Sydney.

Wild, M & Vivas, J (1984) *Wilfred Gordon Macdonald Partridge*. Omnibus, Adelaide.

CHAPTER TWELVE

Taking shape:
Aesthetics and drama form

Drama is a method of teaching and learning, but it's also an art form — one of the ways in which we come to know the world. While an art form (e.g. drama, dance, visual art, music, literature) evolves within a particular culture, the artist has choices. For example, s/he can challenge the way things are (as Anthony Browne does in his portrayal of humans in *Zoo*) or celebrate the way things could be (as Nadia Wheatley does in her depiction of social harmony at the end of *Dancing in the Anzac Deli*). Working in the arts in the primary school means working with feelings and beliefs, and conveying meanings through a variety of forms.

A Statement on the Arts for Australian Schools (1994) points out that students can be art makers, performers, audience members, critics or theorists. So far in this book we've focused on students as makers and performers. But it's also important for them to learn to refine their skills as audience members, whether they're watching the work of classmates, enjoying performances at assemblies, or critically evaluating the presentation of plays by professional actors.

Making and watching

There's no need for a major division between students' activities as makers and audience members; the audience function can be developed in ordinary classroom improvisations. Cecily O'Neill (1995) has pointed out that even while students are actively engaged in a drama, they also have *percipient* roles: that is, while each appears to be fully committed to enacting a role in a fictional world, they are also watching, aware of themselves and their peers pretending. This may involve balancing contradictory emotions, or what Vygotsky (1976:549) called 'dual affect' — "the child weeps in play as a patient, but revels as a player". Two techniques that help students to operate simultaneously as participants and viewers are **role within role** and **protection into role**.

Role within role

A character or event is not always what it seems. O'Neill has remarked that many fairy stories have characters pretending to be someone else (e.g. the wolves in *Red Riding Hood* and *The Three Little Pigs*). Science-fiction and detective stories also use role within role (e.g. Clark Kent really being Superman, or the butler being the murderer). Asking students to enact a role which is itself a role — like a witch pretending to be a good fairy — increases the 'watching' element. Reflection afterwards can consider how they've tried to suggest the ambivalence of the character.

Protection into role

Although the main purpose of protection into role is to establish a healthy distance between the student and a risky enactment (see Chapter 1), it also strengthens the percipient function. For example, you might ask students to spend time drawing and describing a new settlement in space, giving them time to familiarise themselves with the fiction they are creating. This can ease them past emotional blocks that reality might impose, freeing them to look at how the settlers might deal with aliens. During reflection after the enactment, you could help them to recognise some real-world applications of this dramatic analogy — for example, exclusion from tribal friendship groups, or prejudice because of race — that are located under its theme of dealing with difference. Sometimes people who've been to the theatre don't realise further layers of meaning until some time later. The same thing often happens in classroom drama. As David Best (1985:184) observed:

> The peculiar force of learning from a work of art consists in an emotional experience which casts a new light on a situation, revealing what the analogous situation amounts to.

From making to aesthetic understanding

Aesthetic learning starts with consciousness of *form*. That consciousness is developed when the viewer's appreciation is not restricted to content (what is happening), but includes the way that content is realised for dramatic effect.

Gavin Bolton (1984:162) has argued that drama becomes aesthetic learning when children, absorbed at first by drama content, "feel in their bones that somehow the incident is heightened, sharpened, condensed, etc. ... they can learn it is form that makes the simple action significant". He suggests that children first experience a form where the elements of drama have been consciously used to create dramatic art, and then gradually build their awareness of how that form was created. In other words, they move from experience to understanding. However, it's not always possible to put that understanding into words. 'Building awareness' might mean helping students to express the effect of their learning in other ways — by drawing, for instance. Alternatively, they might work slowly with sculpture and discuss it during or after the process.

Creating a performance for others: acting and directing

Teachers are often asked to prepare and present a dramatic item at a school assembly or an end-of-year celebration. Accordingly, the focus of their work shifts from exploratory drama to ways of communicating with an audience. Then, as Bolton says (in Hargreaves, 1990:129), "the actors have to prepare themselves in techniques militating against spontaneity in favour of *repeatability*". Sometimes the material has emerged from the students' own improvised drama; sometimes it's an adaptation of a book; sometimes they act in a play written by a playwright.

Directing

When students are working towards a performance, a directorial role — an outside eye — becomes vital. It is the director who plans the total effect that the performance will have. If the students are inexperienced, the director's task is best left to the teacher to begin with, but it can be shared and gradually handed over. Even school beginners can be asked: "How do we want the audience to feel?" and "I wonder what would make them feel that way?". The director has to stand outside the evolving performance and see it as the audience will see it, adjusting movement, spacing, gestures and so on until each communicates the desired effect. Preparing for performance often means using trial and error to refine what may have been originally created spontaneously; it means rehearsing until the students achieve a finished performance that they can repeat.

One advantage of developing a play from the students' own improvisations is that it engenders feelings of ownership. In addition, links between their experience and the fiction are assured, and the problem of having a few stars and lots of 'spear-carriers' or 'autumn leaves' is avoided. It also makes it easy to incorporate local references — in-jokes, recognisable settings, and characters who appeal because they 'fit' the students enacting them. You can create leading roles for a gymnast or a yodeller (depending on who's in the class!). Playbuilding techniques (described in Chapter 7) can be put to good use here.

Preparing to act

Performances are usually based on a script that has evolved from a class improvisation, or has been written by an established playwright. Students can be assisted to adopt roles and interact with other people in role in order to enact the script for an audience. The most important technique for them to learn is to suspend their disbelief — to explore their character so that it becomes real for them. Therefore, when you begin to interpret a script with your class, you should spend lots of time talking with the group to make the fiction come alive.

Preparatory steps

1. Read the whole play aloud, with class members taking on the roles. At this point you won't have cast the play, but you may be using the interpretations you hear in the readings to help you decide which students are best suited to which roles.
2. Discuss the things that students were most amused by or interested in. Students should explore the fictional world in more depth. For example, they might draw Alison Ashley's bedroom, or bring in objects they think Erica or

Alison would be likely to have. What sort of a pencil case might Erica have in comparison to Alison?

3. Allow lots of time for rehearsal. If you're working with older students, one of them could act as the director for each scene, and take responsibility for the external appearance of the performance.

4. Rather than have only a few 'stars' enacting the script, consider breaking the play into different scenes, with a different cast for each scene. Students could wear an identifying piece of costume to indicate who they are. One person from each group can liaise with the others in order to ensure that the play flows smoothly.

5. Encourage those actors who are to portray the same character to work in expert groups so that they can compare and contrast interpretations of the role — for example, the ways that the character might talk or move, or the attitudes s/he might have to other characters in the play.

6. Consider casting a scene several times, with different casts trying different interpretations. For example, one cast group might stress the comedy; another might put the emphasis on the conflict. (In the scene in *Space Demons* where Elaine meets Mario for the first time, one group might present her as confident and unafraid. Another might stress how intimidating Mario is.) After each group has performed, discuss the differences and similarities.

Reading a script

It's important to realise that reading a dramatic script is a difficult task. Readers are trying to do two things simultaneously. On the one hand, they are reading 'aesthetically', empathising with the characters and events (which mainly involves the dialogue). On the other hand, they are reading for practical information about how the play might be staged.

Scripts are aimed at directors, designers and actors, whose collaboration is required to realise their full meaning. A script is a text *about* a text. Students reading a script need to read for understanding of the action, of course, but they also need to read for information about how to bring a performance before an audience — stage directions, other cues (such as pauses), and details of the set, lighting and costumes. Readers' theatre scripting (discussed in Chapter 9) provides a useful introduction to the nature of script-reading.

Script-reading strategies

- Choose *drama games* that orientate students towards the themes and ideas of the play (see Chapter 2). For instance, a game about being the odd one out (like 'Pig in the Middle') might be useful for a play about Alison Ashley.
- Before reading, set up parallel *improvisations* (i.e. different scenes that will evoke the same emotions).
- Prepare a *reading* of the script using the readers' theatre strategies described in Chapter 9.
- *Hot-seat* a character to build up the background for a scene.
- Set up *still images* to extract the main point of each scene.
- Have the class *sculpt* the characters at a particular moment. They can then talk through what's happening.
- Isolate *key sentences* or *phrases* (e.g. "Erica Yurken, where do you think you're going?") and prepare improvisations that start or end with them.
- Have the class work in *small groups* where individual experts focus on reading the script as a:
  - director
  - actor
  - designer.
- Support students to *draw* each scene, showing where, how and why the characters will move.

Watching others perform: The spectator function

Any successful performance requires the collaboration of the audience, and it could be argued that meaning ultimately resides in the interaction between the spectators and the makers of a performance. Theatre in education (TIE) is a form of professional theatre specially designed for children. Performed by adults, it's usually presented in the audience's school environment. TIE first emerged in England during the 1960s, and the actor-teachers of the Belgrade Theatre in Coventry were the first to use the term. They drew on many of the same principles as Dorothy Heathcote, actively involving their audience by asking for suggestions on how to solve dilemmas and absorbing the answers into the flow of the play. TIE set out to teach about theatre as well as teaching particular content.

In Australia, TIE teams like Toe Truck, Magpie, Salamanca, Freewheels and Zeal have made it their mission to bring good theatre to schools, and part of their practice has been to work with students after a performance, assisting in deconstruction of the play. Inviting such companies to your school is a good way to induct students into the experience of theatre, and to teach them how to be a good audience.

Recently, writers who have worked in TIE have begun to publish scripts of their plays (e.g. David Holman's *No Worries* and *Small Poppies*). As these were devised for adult actors, they're probably too difficult for your students to perform complete, although selected scenes are feasible. Other playwrights have adapted successful children's novels as plays: for instance, Richard Tulloch has dramatised *Hating Alison Ashley* and *Space Demons*, and there are scripts of *Boss of the Pool* (by Mary Morris) and *Puppy Love* (by Bruce Keller).

The experience of watching any theatrical performance is enhanced by discussion afterwards. Students need to talk about how they felt while they were watching, and how they feel now. Given the opportunity to discuss constructively the way a performance was staged (and why), and how certain characters were portrayed, they will come to understand better the role of the audience in drama.

How we felt

We asked some students how they felt about drama performances they could remember. Some of these memories last a long time ...

Thirteen-year-old Lucy made these comments about a play she had seen.

> I remember going to performances by 'Image Theatre' when I was quite small. I remember we saw the story of 'Columbine and Harlequin'. They used shadow puppetry to tell part of the story. I loved it and the acting was so good I believed it really happened ... the costumes were so colourful, too.

Beau's thoughts about the musical of *The Lion King* also focused on the visual.

> I just thought it was good all round. My favourite characters were Scar and the Hyenas because they were so funny. The costuming was great. I loved the way they built Cheetah – the strings were attached to its neck so that you really thought it was a Cheetah's head when it moved.

References and sources

Australian Education Council (1994) *A Statement on the Arts for Australian Schools*. Curriculum Corporation, Melbourne.

Best, D (1985) *Feeling and Reason in the Arts*. Allen & Unwin, London.

Browne, A (1992) *Zoo*. Julia MacRae Books, London.

Holman, D (1984) *No Worries*. Currency Press, Sydney.

Holman, D (1986) *Small Poppies*. Currency Press, Sydney.

Hargreaves, D (1990) *Children and the Arts*. Open University Press, Milton Keynes.

Keller, B (1991) *Puppy Love*. Unpublished TS, Toetruck Theatre, Sydney.

Klein, R (1984) *Hating Alison Ashley*. Puffin Books, Melbourne.

Klein, R (1988) *The Play: Hating Alison Ashley*. Adapted for the stage by Richard Tulloch. Puffin Books, Australia.

Morris, M (1993) *Boss of the Pool: Adapted for the Stage*. Currency Press, Sydney.

O'Neill, C (1995) *Drama Worlds: A Framework for Process Drama*. Heinemann, London.

Rubenstein, G (1986) *Space Demons*. Penguin Books, Australia.

Rubenstein, G (1990) *Space Demons: The Play*. Adapted for the stage by Richard Tulloch, Omnibus, Adelaide.

Vygotsky, L (1976) *Thought and Language*. MIT Press, Cambridge, MA.

Wheatley, N (1986) *Dancing in the Anzac Deli*. Oxford, Australia.

EPILOGUE

Imagination is central to children's learning. The list of theorists and writers who have advocated the centrality of the imagination in education seems endless (Dewey, Piaget, Vygotsky, Bruner, Barnes, Britton, Rosen, Smith, Greene, Egan, to name only a few). Bruner (1990) asserts that our capacity to create, both in science and in narrative, *depends* on our ability to imagine; Egan (2003) suggests that we have too often begun with what children already know, rather than what they can imagine.

The potential of the arts to enhance students' learning across all learning areas seems to be taking on a new importance in Canada and the United States. Sadly, in Australia to date, this potential for the arts in general — and drama in particular — to open up the meanings of our everyday experience, make new connections and uncover new possibilities remains undervalued.

It's our hope that this book has demonstrated how dramatic play enables your students to enter imaginatively into different experiences and to explore the ambiguity and contradictions of the world we live in. Perhaps more than ever before, our students need opportunities to view the world from others' perspectives. Only then will educational aspirations to promote greater understanding, tolerance and peace become more than rhetoric.

Educational drama is far more than a 'box of tricks' or a fun lesson-filler, only good for providing a motivational lead into 'real' learning about what can be measured or solved. The cross-curricular drama strategies described in this book can foster the development of our students' imaginations and help them grow in their understanding of different perspectives and meanings. It can also help them to envisage potential changes, solve problems in creative ways, and ask the big life questions such as 'How can I live well with my neighbour?'.

Do you still feel tentative about teaching drama? We all carry baggage from our past experiences. Many of us seem to carry excess luggage from our experiences of the school play. However, we can no longer afford to ignore the possibilities that dramatic processes open up across the curriculum. The only way to overcome apprehension is to make a start, however tentative. Some of the early chapters in this book suggest ways in which you might do this: beginning with movement, mime or still image; setting clear guidelines and expectations for the activities; engaging in open discussion with students about your purposes; and setting aside time for reflection afterwards. Certainly, once launched, we're sure you'll find that drama activities are the most powerful teaching and learning strategies of all, and that your journey will be exciting and rewarding.

BRIEF GLOSSARY

Elements of drama

The teacher needs to select content using these four elements.

Role
Not only acting; it is adopting the attitudes of another person, and temporarily suspending disbelief. A role may be specific or general, stereotypical or three-dimensional. The choice of roles may determine the ideology of the drama.

Tension
Prevention of a resolution. May be created by using space, time, motivation, conflict, contrast etc.

Symbol
Anything that stands for something else (e.g. for an object, person, concept, emotion or state of mind). The most fruitful drama is where a specific incident or object reflects a more general situation.

Focus
Narrows attention to a specific question: what are you most interested in investigating?

Levels of role

1. Dramatic playing	Students are themselves in an imaginary situation.
2. Mantle of the expert	Students become 'the ones who know'.
3. Role-playing	Students adopt attitudes which are not necessarily their own.
4. Characterising	Students adopt the characteristics of a particular individual.
5. Acting	Students rehearse and present to an audience.

Drama devices

Collective drawing Students in small groups design an image together.

Conscience alley The role/character walks slowly between two lines of students facing each other, who comment in role or tell the character what s/he should do.

Defining space	Furniture and material used to represent a place.
Depiction	Still image or frozen moment; use of bodies to crystallise an interaction.
De-roling	The process of stepping back out of role.
Drama games	Childhood games put into a particular context.
Freeze frame	A particular dramatic moment that has been frozen to allow close study. Also known as *tableau*.
Hot-seating	Questioning selected student/s, in role, by seating them in front of the class group. Aimed at building roles, not interrogating. Also known as *questioning in role*.
Improvisation	Unscripted drama; words and actions are invented spontaneously.
Mantle of expert	Students are given high-status roles as experts in a drama.
Mime	Expressive gesture with no words.
Readers' theatre	Narrative scripting leading to group story-telling; emphasis on voice and limited gesture.
Ritual	Stylised enactment with rules and codes.
Role-on-the-wall	An important role is drawn on paper; individuals write words or longer comments to define it. They may then each speak for it.
Sculpting	Participants use the body of another as 'thinking clay', shaping it to represent a significant moment, negotiating things like expressions.
Soundscape	A sequence of sound effects created by voices or instruments to evoke a mood, image or set of images.
Teacher in role	Teacher takes on a role and manages interactions and direction from within the drama.
Telephone conversations	One-way conversations with an imagined other.
Thought-tracking	'Tapping in' to reveal what is being thought at a point in time. Often used in combination with depiction.
Unfinished materials	Objects introduced as a starting point for role creation.

SELECTED FURTHER DRAMA REFERENCES

Baldwin, P & Fleming, K (2003) *Teaching Literacy through Drama*. Routledge Falmer, London.

Boal, A (1979) *The Theatre of the Oppressed*. Pluto Press, London.

Burton, B (1991) *The Act of Learning*. Longman Cheshire, Melbourne.

Charters, J & Gately, A (1987) *Drama Anytime*. Primary English Teaching Association, Sydney.

Cusworth, R (1991) 'Using Readers' Theatre to Explore Text Form'. In McKay, F (ed.), *Public and Private Lessons: The Language of Teaching and Learning*. Australian Reading Association, Melbourne.

Fleming, M (1994) *Starting Drama Teaching*. David Fulton, London.

Haseman, B (1986) *Dramawise: An Introduction to the Elements of Drama*. Heinemann, Melbourne.

Haseman, B & O'Toole, J (1987) *Dramawise*. Heinemann, Melbourne.

Heathcote, D & Bolton, G (1995) *Drama for Learning*. Heinemann, Melbourne.

Hertzberg, M & Ewing, R (1998) 'Developing Our Imagination: Enactment and Critical Literacy'. *PEN* 116. Primary English Teaching Association, Sydney.

Hughes, J (ed.) (1991) *Drama in Education: The State of the Art*. Educational Drama Association, Sydney.

Kempe, A (2001) 'Drama as a Framework for the Development of Literacy. *Set* 2.

McMaster, J (1998) 'Doing Literature: Using Drama to Build Literacy'. *The Reading Teacher* 51.

Moore, T (ed.) *Phoenix Texts: A Window on Drama Practice in Australian Primary Schools*. National Association for Drama in Education, Melbourne.

Morgan, N & Saxton, J (1994) *Asking Better Questions*. Pembroke, Ontario.

Neelands, J (1993) *Structuring Dramawork*. Cambridge University Press, Cambridge.

NSW Department of Education and Training (1998) *Exploring the Worlds of K–6 Drama: From Ancient Anna to the Cloth of Dreams*. Inc. video. NSW DET, Sydney.

NSW Department of Education and Training (2002) *Arts Action: A Resource to Support Teachers Implementing the NSW Creative Arts Syllabus*. NSW DET, Sydney.

O'Mara, J (2003) 'Repositioning Drama to Centrestage: Drama, English, Text and Literacy'. *Drama Australia Journal* 27(2).

O'Neill, C (1995) *Dramaworlds: A Framework for Process Drama*. Heinemann, London.

O'Neill, C & Rogers, T (1994) 'Drama and Literary Response: Prying Open the Text, *English in Australia* 108.

O'Neill, C (1982) *K–6 Drama Structures: A Practical Handbook for Teachers*. Hutchinson, London.

O'Toole, J & Dunn, J (2002) *Pretending to Learn*. Pearson, Melbourne.

Pierse, L (1993) *Theatresports Downunder*. Improcorp, Sydney.

Robertson, M (1990) 'True Wizardry'. *PEN* 79. Primary English Teaching Association, Sydney.

Simons, J (in press) 'Playbuilding: More than the Sum of the Parts'. In Mooney, M & Nicholls J (eds), *Drama Journey: Inside Drama Learning*, Currency Press, Sydney.

Simons, J (1989) 'Playbuilding: Theory and Practice'. *Do It! Journal of NSW Educational Drama Association* 45.

Simons, J & Bateman P (2000) 'Developing Collaborative Creativity'. *Drama Australia* 24 (1).

Simons, J & Quirk, L (1991) 'Standing up the Text: Using Drama to Teach Literature'. In Fumiss, L & Green, P (eds), *The Literacy Connection*. Eleanor Curtain Publishing, Melbourne.

Smigiel, H (ed.) (1991) *Drama Down Under*. NADIE, Adelaide.

Spurgeon, D (1991) *From Improvisation to Dance*. Harcourt Brace Jovanovich, Sydney.

Taylor, P (2000) *The Drama Classroom: Action Reflection Transformation*. Routledge, New York.

Winston, J & Tandy, M (1998) *Beginning Drama 4–11*. Fulton, London.

Website

Drama Australia
www.dramaustralia.org.au